FLIPSTONES

Jim Mackintosh

FLIPSTONES

New and Selected Poems

Jim Mackintosh

TIPPERMUIR
· BOOKS LIMITED ·

This first edition published and copyright 2018 by
Tippermuir Books Ltd, Perth, Scotland.

mail@tippermuirbooks.co.uk

www.tippermuirbooks.co.uk

The Publisher is not responsible for websites (or their content) that are
not owned by the Publisher.

Editorial and Project Management: Paul S. Philippou.
Project Support: Jean Hands and Rob Hands.
Cover design: Matthew Mackie.

ISBN: 978-0-9954623-8-0 (paperback).

A CIP catalogue record for this book is available from the British Library.

Text styling and artwork by Bernard Chandler [graffik], Glastonbury, England.
Text set in DIN FF Regular 9.5 on 15 pt. and DIN FF Bold.

Printed in Great Britain by CPI Group (UK) Ltd, Croydon CR0 4YY.

"Jim is a diehard St Johnstone fan and makes an important contribution to the cultural fabric of Perthshire."

John Swinney Deputy First Minister of Scotland

"Jim's writing reveals how poetry can engage us with the everyday and the known and at the same time nudge us toward recognising the often harder to articulate range of human experiences like toil, playfulness and an appreciation of the sublime. His poems about landscapes capture their ancient drama and life-giving power and bring their people and places into a new focus for our times."

Clare Cooper, co-producer, Cateran's Common Wealth

"When an artist's film ignites the imagination of a poet, we are in receipt of a gift – a poetic acclaim like no other. 'Landlocked' works of art from a museum collection of contemporary art such as **To the End of the Fingertips** suddenly become alive and free, almost able to fly off the screen and unfold the page as in Mackintosh's **Paper Bones**."

"With Mackintosh's **Toned Genuflection** one almost bends a knee in poetic respect to the dance and voice artists, aka those 'keepers of movement', as featured in the inspiring artist's film **Pilgrimage**. We travel along the Way 'where ash road patterns pass windmills brooding, like vacant crosses'; where rhythm is like light for the footsteps whether in sun's glare or in moon-lit darkness."

"**Tailored** – an ultra-short artist's film is complemented by the lapidarium of a poem in Mackintosh's **Spun Glimpses**. Poem and film become a 'mirror of our own fragile truths' composed of broken hearts, cursive glimpses, 'measured dance' and 'stitching impulses'."

"When the endearing and enduring genre of self-portraiture captures the corner of the poetic eye as in Mackintosh's **Floral Print Axe**, we emerge wiser and wilder 'separating the worthless from the worth'. Our 'we' merges with the 'I' from the **Self-Portrait**, as we stand, in between the artists' metaphors and their 'aesthetic muscles', and we almost hear the exploding 'drumbeat heart' of art and life."

Iliyana Nedkova Curator and Writer,
Creative Director of Contemporary Art at Horsecross Arts, Perth

read a poem

touch it

write a poem

feel it

recite a poem

inhale it

breathe a poem

live it

:be the poem:

for all my family
for all my friends
including you

Karen.

Fair chuffes tae tel ye.
Muckle joy on yer day!

Jim.

18/09/2018

Jim Mackintosh

Photo by Dave Hunt

http://www.silveralchemy.co.uk

The Silver Alchemy Collective is about capturing
photographic images in the traditional manner.
Coming from a time when we gave space to
consider our subject, a time when the image had
more importance then the process, a time when
we truly understood the relevance of photography
as a means to capture a moment to be kept forever.

ACKNOWLEDGEMENTS & NOTES

Beneath the Glass - inspired by the discovery of a long cist burial at Bridge of Tilt, near Blair Atholl, in 1986 and the subsequent exhibition of the finds at Perth Museum & Art Gallery in 2017, which included a digital reconstruction of a 'Pictish Man' using remains found at the site.

Broken - features on an installation of the Corbenic Poetry Path (near Dunkeld).

Carpow - inspired by the excavation of a 3,000-year-old logboat from the River Tay at Carpow and the permanent exhibition of the logboat at Perth Museum & Art Gallery.

Floral Print Axe - commissioned by Threshold Artspace to mark the digital art installation of *Selma Selman* when it was shown as part of Platform Festival (Perth) 2017.

Griz an Cateran - commissioned by The Soldiers Charity to mark The Cateran Yomp 2017; performed at the pre-event 'Briefings'.

Innerpeffray - inspired by Innerpeffray Library (near Crieff). Founded around 1680, Innerpeffray Library is the oldest free public lending library in Scotland.

It Used to be Bottles - appeared in the pamphlet *#Refugees Welcome* (Eyewear Books, 2015).

James: A King in Waiting and Last Order - inspired by the Charterhouse Project and the quest to trace the tombs of King James I of Scotland and his queen Joan of Beaufort.

Rituals and **Turnstiles** - appeared in *Mind the Time* (Backpage Press, 2017), an anthology of football related poetry edited by Jim Mackintosh; produced to support the work of Football Memories Scotland.

The Bicycle - appeared in the pamphlet *#NousSommesParis* (Eyewear Books, 2016) on the first anniversary of the November 2015 Paris attacks.

Terra Nullius and **Wisdom's Juice** - both commissioned by Artipeeps and Cambridge University; appeared as part of a multi-layered art exhibition based on the 'Nine Realms of the Norse Gods' in Norfolk in 2015.

The following poems emerged from a collaboration with Iliyana Nedkova, the Creative Director of Contemporary Art at Horsecross Arts, Perth, and the exhibition 11 Million Reasons to Dance.

Dance Essence - a series of three poems inspired the exhibition as a whole and by Iliyana whose energy, knowledge, generosity, and enthusiasm inflames a creativity to explore fresh words and to work collaboratively.

Denial Steps - inspired by Augenblick's (Italy) 2016 dance art film *Tailored*.

Paper Bones - inspired by Roswitha Chesher's 2017 dance art film *To the End of the Fingertips*.

Toned Genuflection - inspired by Marlene Millar's 2017 dance art film *Pilgrimage*.

The following poems developed from a residency at Platform Festival (Perth) 2018 and were inspired by connections made during the festival with other artists and their work.

Gunpowder Leap and Butterfly Gallery - inspired by the works of contemporary figurative painter Frank To. Having studied art at the University of Huddersfield, Frank refined his craft at Duncan of Jordanstone Art College. He works out of his studio in Glasgow. The insect pieces in the festival exhibition, including the butterfly which inspired the poem, were a response to Frank's research into the natural and community history of Perth & Kinross; from analysing insect specimens Frank realised how important bees, moths, and butterflies are to the eco-system. The exhibition provided an opportunity for the viewing of Frank's art without budgetary restriction and demonstrated the importance of the craft of drawing through the provision of an artist residency at Perth Museum & Art Gallery.

Shore Road Coral - inspired by Susie Johnston's sculpture *Circle of Circles*. This piece emerged through an artist residency with the Binn Group (Perth), which provided Susie with an opportunity to use waste materials and to realise her yearning to learn to weld. Susie's sculptural work for some time had been inspired by a belief that all 'matter' whether animate or inanimate embodies a vibrancy. The residency celebrated and embraced principles of a circular rather than linear economy. The Binn Group provided a space to work, a welder and generator, and access to welding training. Susie spent two months sourcing ferrous and non-ferrous metals; responding to objects that she knew nothing about. The residency enabled Susie to create new sculptural works through a process of sandblasting, welding, and angle grinding. From these discarded objects Susie was able to release new meaning from their re-presentation within the context of Perth Museum & Art Gallery and as public art located by the entrance to the Binn Group's Shore Road site, which provided the catalyst for the poem.

Silver Alchemy - inspired by the work of the Silver Alchemy Collective and the photograph taken using a traditional 'wet plate collodion' process by collective member Dave Hunt.

Tak Tent - inspired by Helen McCrorie's 2018 short film *Against The Flow*, based on the flood which affected Comrie and the challenges residents faced to recover personal memories or reconcile themselves with their permanent loss.

Twa Chiels - inspired by an afternoon by the River Ericht (Blairgowrie) with artist Aileen Stackhouse. *'Everyone is an artist said Joseph Beuys and I believe this is true. The creative impulse is within all of us, imagination is essential for basic mundane everyday life from making a meal to planning a journey from beans on toast to apple pie from getting the bus home to flying off on a mystery tour we have become separated from the world by our advanced technology when all we need is art, a pencil, a pen, a guitar, our hands, our eyes, our ears, our voices the freedom to move within the world and the landscapes of our imagination.'* Aileen Stackhouse.

CONTENTS

from

'MIND THE TIME' and the
ST JOHNSTONE F.C. RESIDENCY

NEW POEMS

from

'TREACLED VEINS'

This Old Tune

An old tune. An assured tap of fingers.
A slow creep o gangrel intentions
ower foggit ground, peat water lingers
licking the toes of weary travellers.

I am looking at the short fuse
of a day, the same day through which
I picked out the rhythm of old blues
in verses I never quite understood.

Up from the undergrowth, midwinter
makes its presence felt, in thin hope
assured in its step, sure slick in rags
gathered at the waist by tarry rope

on which the remains of autumn drop
in solemn, flopped surrender, necks
snapped in hard judgement, skin flop
gutted and ready for the boiling pot.

My assured landscape, aa *howk backit*
under the weight of binding roots
treacle vein slowed by a single knot,
the last dampness of familiar shoots

clogs in the bottle neck, memories lost
piling up in a bulge of pulped adventures
but the words creep upwards through frost
to poke the ribs of the shortened gloom.

Because we will determine the incarnation
of our dreams, wine dark, blushed pink,
nibbed with the finest diamonds of ambition
to work the Gods into the release of Spring.

One More Try

Give it a try -
what does that look like?
- that try, that consumption of effort
to bridge a gap, to query the gait
and break the stride of normal.

To reach out, to hold, to accept
to embrace the stunning reality
that your bubble, our shared world
was built on trying - on success and failure.
There's an ancient oak rooted in my mind,

its branches stretching out their muscles
to all the horizons of my yesterdays
- that I, at some point – foolishly, effortlessly
or whilst insanely drunk tried, somehow
succeeded to walk beyond my thin horizon.

This joyous oak of a thousand brightly coloured
silk rags, each one knotted, tied with care
to a gnarled branch recording my tries,
all my efforts, reminding me
that none were failures.

I have a bag, a carpet bag
made from my Granny's hearthside rug,
where I would sit in awe of her,

watch her wise hands make silk rags
brightly coloured threads of wisdom
which I keep in the carpet bag
in my mind, for one more try.

There's room on the high branches for a rag.
There's always one more horizon,
to go beyond and hold out a hand,
to take a hand, to hold, to embrace
one more try - there's always room
for one more try.

The Blue Lit Roads

I have no conscious memory of my crime.
I have neither stamp of guilt nor lick of flame.
No mark of retribution borne on my flesh.

The clouds seized my limbs and lashed them
To the sharp shoulders of this dark glen,
Where the Three Sisters disembowelled me

For my entrails to fuse into the high tide
Those pointless exercises of human form
Unnecessary in the mizzle soothing my lips.

The comforting soft rain on my shoulders
And everywhere, blue light on the sea roads
Where fear has no name in the tide turn.

And me, waiting on the story boats tilt
Into the shadowed pier to release my memory
From the bind of covenant by which I'm damned.

I have no conscious memory of my crime.
I have only the scars of my love for you.
I have only the damp earth choking my lungs.

If you would spend one day in this land
It'd pull your heart into its forgiving grip
And love all of you, flaws and all forever.

If you'll take my hand and let your sadness go
I'll pull the tides behind us until the blue light
Guides and folds its comfort safely around us.

The Leaf

It lay there exhausted.
Death had sucked the juice from
treacled veins – curves curled
with a nibbled edge
alone
on the oak panelled floor
- the kinship of an oak leaf.

They say it's not the fall
that kills you.
Does it?
I lifted the fallen.
The fragile, drained body close
to my body, and into my notebook
where I write these words.

An obituary
respectfully around us
and a single leaf
lifeless yet
alive forever more
in the fold of a page, and a poem
nurtured by its sacrifice.

The Distillery Path

I think about you and the summer of back then.
Scuffing the warmth of holidays - I was fifteen.
I remember the dusty veined path beaten flat.
along the Distillery wall by the narrow pines
where the sinews of mash hypnotised innocence.

There was a point I daren't cross – an oak root stop.
Ahead an impenetrable wall of barbed mystery.
Through the bricks of malted air – bustling monks
amid hushed sparks of amber, prayed and blessed.
Not everyone could hear them whisper their secrets.

The emerald tipped manicure of Arthur Bell's Palace,
a no-man's land with hosannahs of geraniums, like
half submerged golden alligators waiting if I dared
approach the black ended walls of holy Bonds beyond,
and the vaulted silence of the Kings at rest - *uisge beatha*.

Somewhere, in the ordered chaos putting up flack
deep in the musk heavy calm rows of casks, congregated
in their regiments of vanilla oak warriors, with
bellies full of nectar turning the years in peace
like beached walrus bound with belts of iron

unaware of day or night to rest in the musty depths
awaiting their call to arms on some distant gantry.
I'd watch enraptured, the leathered apron approach
the High Priest, boots like boulders and steps of thunder.
He dared to enter the inner sanctum - silence.

Muffled knocks of unknown rituals - oak on oak,
prayers in muted code to the Barley Kings of Summer.
Apron returns with a wipe of granite chin, dram sweet.
There must've been a sacrifice - I was converted.
My calling sealed - *Sláinte Mhaith* - I promised.

Calvie

In May 1845, ninety people were evicted, conned from their homes in Glen Calvie, Sutherland, Scotland. Forced to seek shelter in the graveyard of Croick Kirk to await their fate, some scratched their names into the church windows - desperate and frightened with an uncertain future ahead.

Fae the siller birk on the far side a movement,
the cuckoo announces the forgotten quarters
as it would have to the wicked generation
of Glen Calvie's honest grafters, terrible innocence
herded like the sheep soon to replace them,
desperately cooried amongst the headstones,
the resting place of ancestors in equal turmoil.

Centuries of sighs seeping up hush-hush, sobbing
through the green velvet oasis of Croick Kirk's acre
offering only an embrace to the sorrowed plight
of the tricked generation of Calvie's lazy bed runs.

Even now the air hangs heavy with sadness, despair
of their innocent crimes, of toil, honesty and kinship.
The original sin loosened from the greedy Factor's grip,
who stabbed hearts evicted for a distant Master's coin.

The lead framed diamonds etched now in mizzled glass
the words of their names, their desperate innocence.
Precious gems of those long departed, defeated yet
remembered now, as the cuckoo announces the quarters
to weave the bitter tone – never forget what they suffered.

Come To Me Another Time Soon
After 18 September 2014

There's an oddness in the day, an air of confused nothing
of ordered silence but for the confident tick of the clock
on the mantelpiece next to the calendar with the red circled 18.
It's like New Year's Day but mournfully sober.

The house is spotless, all neat and tidy, bowls of peanuts
and those fancy nibbles the ones the young folk like.
Crumbed Ham from the Butchers and an extra loaf
in case they brought friends, and a tin of salmon in the cupboard
but there was an oddness in the night.

The hours passed with jigsaw snippets of an odd laugh
a strangled cheer but no hurrahs, an occasional glance
at the door and at the clock on the mantelpiece
next to the calendar with the red circled 18.
The peanuts sat, we watched the programmes
until they didn't mean anything beyond –

the point of relevance to the party that hadn't started,
the doorbell that hadn't rung and a last hopeful peak beyond
the curtains at the lights on at the neighbour's three down
where it seemed the majority were ringing in the changes
pledged of nothing beyond the price of crumbed ham.

There's an oddness in the day, sitting here folding ham sandwiches
into a ballot box, in the grub of the non-circled 19.
The dying embers in the fire stoked for the party that didn't come
to me but went to the neighbour's three doors down
beyond the storm of sparrows eating peanuts on the lawn.

from

'BOTTLING THE BEEPS'

Grasping the Rose

Softly, softly crossing the weave
yet so far, so softly far away.
Love me, gentle spirit, love me
find me here in the nook of a day

where your voice holds the still
through the calm of a poisonous chill,
and rumours starch the berry wood
with the ruby kiss of witches' blood

staining clouds on the emerald loch
with spells found in the maiden's broch
where scolding irons jammed the door
and her heart burned bitter on the floor.

The words are wrong, the days are long
between us, the birds drown in song
washed out of storms bubbled swell
drift-feathers under her broken spell

I'm no nearer solving your mystery.
I'm no braver in grasping the rose
so I'll kiss the lips of the martyr'd briar
where our dying breaths still compose.

Making Space

and in the clear sky, the faintest hint
of parallel lines, autumn's manuscript
unfolding across a late summer day

circled days of adventures and celebrations
falling from the calendar, wandering
aimlessly about the desk, uncertain

where to go. To what should they cling to
in the faultless decline of sun's blessing?
So few days to find safety in a bowl

amongst tokens and vouchers for days out
unaware their expiry dates have doomed
their crumple to the flirtation of bonfires

stoked with the splintered fragments
of a garden with ache, falling from trees
unburdened across a late summer day

On This Day For Half Roads
For Boston

we walked the length of half roads
and sat on the kerbs, dismissing death
in the passing stillness of blue tides
and we became part of the landscape

like the moon, pulling and pushing
at our futures, the power to terrify
or light the shimmer of dappled hours
where summer kisses the honey lips

of soft winds, and love tangles
rainbows in your hair, as the breath
of nature's grace danced across a face
with a smile you'd won at the fair

but the gears of the Ferris wheel seized
when destiny tripped us up, bluntly
laughing at the dust bowl grimace
drifting across the innocence of strangers

limbs, powerless to change direction
on a morning of impossible heroes
running into the storm, devouring
fear with the dark eclipse of hatred

clawing at their faces, no quarter
yet no one stopped, no one slept
and in the moonlight the landscape
spilled from our open hearts

it was the day of terrible things
the toil of twisted reality, bursting
through the dappled shade of trees
catching the shreds of the emptying day

but none of those lost were forgotten
when we stood up at the bloody kerb
and walked down the half-roads of sorrow
together, to win another smile at the fair

Elsie

No need to knock. At most, softly on the door then go quietly in
The hush of days counted down in pencil, red circled in bold
Of not much else but one ambition – fussed and royally appointed
A calendar by a fireplace, its glow toasting memories wearing thin
A bundle of knitted simplicity, Elsie alone, no longer feeling old
Days short of One Hundred, content to reach it less the fuss anointed
By the Queen to hand over the Telegram, to pose for the media prize
With Elsie who will raise a smile – just, but inwardly biting her tongue
They don't know this strong woman who trekked from China to India
To survive the churn of bloody war, nurse, missionary – her true eyes
Beyond knowing, unless they ask, and they won't. Once they've sung
The Song and the crumbs of fuss brushed away, in the hush not too far
Of no longer counted or circled bold days, Elsie will sit alone and wait.
So chap an Elsie's door across a road from you. Don't leave it late.

The Dotted Line

A day of terms and conditions
even the sky must sign
on the dotted line

held steady in the wind
where the horizon
suspends the hours

weatherless
motionless

until you read the small print
drawn in the sand
birdsong bottling up
in the long grass
speared to the back shore.

A blur of resistance
escapes through the sapless fence
a gap in the contract
a loophole of memory

tossed into the air
hooked on the spinach weed
which defines the tide's ambition.

I'm sitting now in the dunes
rehearsing my words
the Covenant earthed
and bound to my sanity.

I sign on the dotted line of another day.

Forbidden Rainbows

Why is there still such a thing as forbidden love?
Somehow shamed – denied its chosen caress
A heart bound, locked in a chest without a key
The love for another safe, beyond scrawny cove
Of scrutiny – judgmental ravens demand to confess
Possession of a rainbow, unfurled, bright and free
Draped on the shoulders of your lover by sweet Liberty
Its ribbons of chosen freedom, a passionate embrace
Ignoring the walls of crumbling, broken spite
Damn the spume of that ragged, blinded trinity
Timendi causa est nescire – declared with grace
Ignorance is the cause of fear – walk into the light
Untie your bonds and let tomorrow's rainbows soar
Beyond Forbidden's walls – hearts tethered no more.

Replenish

Sit with me in this soft sigh of Spring,
no closer than my trampled breath
has allowed since the slump of air
left the lungs of winter's remains.
I will re-invent our future days.

Come. Whisper no longer from a distance.
The sun has lifted ill from the stale field
to freshen the days again with blossom
and your footsteps amongst the blink
of warm horizons will be my blessing.

We will embroider the hills together.
You, in a coat of polished granite and
I, in the finest bluebell shoes, scented
with the passion of replenished land
where the snows have slipped away.

from

'EIGHT ROWS BACK'

A Woman with a Dead Banana

I saw a woman this morning carrying a dead banana
by the tip of its potential
lifeless now, discoloured,
like the tragic flop of unexpected road kill.

She crossed the road seemingly intent on dragging out
the public humiliation of this flaccid wretch
like the bitter scraps of the gallow snap
depriving the raven its scraps of discard.

She caught me watching and smeared my part
in this unscripted drama with a smile
of such acidic intensity as if to say
'Don't mess with me or you're next'

I bowed my head and walked on
with the mock of ravens ringing in my mind.
Why should I care about bananas anyway?
They're not from around here. I'm ashamed.

The Gardening Jacket

my grandad's tweed jacket
shaped by the seasons
held together, filled by fragments of him

a penknife, bone handled, the silver inlay lost
the memories of string of cabbages snicked fresh

loose tobacco trapped into corners
enough for two fills
hiding from the reality the pipe was snapped

the cobbled stitch of a plaid patch
on an elbow worn from fence post leans

the sweet, unknown air folding through me
like the memory of a piper's lament

on the walk, solemn paced to the Kirkyard
leaving the jacket on the shed door

for cabbages and days of yellow broom sprigs
where drills of seed fill the pockets with him

This Was My Landscape

this was my [**landscape**]

the landscape that walks up
sits right next to me unannounced, silent
yet welcome to sit with a stranger

on choking days
on neon nights

there are no mountains
no waterfalls
no snow
unless you want it cut in a deal bag
which will melt your soul

there's concrete
there's marble
there are people
thousands, blinkered
and me, a stranger
yet belonging

this was my [**landscape**]

there's noise

:white noise:
:dark noise:

the hurry of strangers
the flight of lovers
the scurry of deaths

in the quiet hours when the stranger
gets up and walks away from me

lost in the noise
folding into the marble
consumed by the concrete

:choking days:
:neon nights:

when I'd ask myself

'what are you doing here?'

and I'd pause, squint into the haze
trace the mountains, inhale the waterfall
taste the snow

:choking days:
:neon nights:

and I'd consume a little more
of the welcome stranger
who has sat beside me
until I could breathe no more

that was my [**landscape**]

A Pale Blue Dot

the curtain in the building across the alley tight
between our existence   has been knotted
    in the middle
of a dead window
for at least a thousand funerals

its peeling frame long since past giving a shit
who sees its blisters exposed
    to crosstown snobbery

its building has slumped in the sad reflection
of its past glories, ornate
but now weighing heavily
in the rudeness of moss pasted to its cherubs
and copper stained tears
of abandoned years flooding
from the burst of a high-top drainpipe

yet, there is an oasis of green, plants hanging
breathing from the rim of a wire basket
risking the fresh passing breeze
oblivious to the rattle of death
in the bricks and mortar
    and the moss choked cherubs

but there in the stifle
    a pale blue dot, shining
        a sweet blue viola

holding out a petal, a hand to be held, to be saved
its life acknowledged by a fragrant existence
straining from the shadows
hoping to be rescued
before the walls are torn down
when the glass explodes and the final curtain falls -

and the knot unravels
in the stagnant air of solitude
sweet, precious pale blue dot
you're worth more than that
take my hand
you must grow
you must flourish in the warmth
of tomorrow's sun

It's Necessary Sometimes

It's necessary sometimes

[**for me**]

maybe you, to muffle the soaring ache of impossible passion, doomed
to walk past the open door of unexpected consequence

writing nothing: bleeding everything

comfortably imprisoned by the scrape of time gorging on my existence
with the death kiss of leeches on my eyelids

swollen: distended

plugging the gaps of slow poison seeping through the cracks of tombstones
in the hours crumbling the words of peace carved across the daylight.

It's necessary sometimes
where passers-by walk by occasionally kneeling down to kiss the mortal slab
of reason by the coolness of water floating the remains of winter downstream
circling in the eddy of currents determined to drown me.

they can't hear my voice
they can't feel my breath
they can only wipe away blood
they can only read my words

It's necessary sometimes

[for us]

to let the leeches explode on the cotton and linen of the
    bloodthirsty masses
who pass by occasionally to check for a pulse or to nose at the
    tombstones

It's necessary sometimes

to stand against the eddy and replenish the supply of

[slow release poison]

from

'PASSING PLACES'

The Skim of Pasts

I had turned into my Grandfather
without a hint of protest, standing
in second best suit trousers neat
with rolled up precision to knees
now mirrored in the lap of soft waves
annoyed by my presence, diverting
their fold on to the empty shore.

I lacked the collarless shirt and pipe
to finish the transition, the boundary
of his effort to blend into the holiday
fuss and feathers of unnecessary joy
bounding and laughing around him,
yet there he stood in the shallows
like me now, feeling for roundies

with bare toes in to the cold sand
like a cake mixture for beach days.
Those polished pebbles, the best ones
capable of a fiver, the perfect skim
and bounce leaving only five quiet circles
rippling outwards across the shimmer
like a dragon fly kissing a silvered mirror.

And then I felt it. With a sideways glance
to hide my plans, I reached down
breaching the surface to lift my prize
a sure winner, a cold space-saucer stone
cupped in my hands, letting the plunge
of silver drip through my fingers, content
in the wade back to the shore, the start

for the next round of the skimmings
concealing my prize, the fiver warming
in my pocket, too cold and it would sink.
I skimmed and watched the dragonfly
dance towards the horizon - one step through
to five and it was gone, returning to wait
for the next generation of rolled up trousers.

Ants and Jam

There is an assurance. A strength of
freshly washed purpose held in the drill
of rain on an innocent summer's day.
Those cloud burst days of certainty
arriving in the corrugated scatter above
like steel hatted ants crossing the roof
on a route march towards certain death,
flushed down the pipe, next to the window
where green tomatoes ripen unaware.

I would sit there in anticipation by
the melamine dresser, lime and bold
of nooks and crannies, and brass top jars
and my mum making jam, raspberry jam
watching her effortless toil comforted
in the claggy sugar spun air and a candy floss
volcano bubbling up the secrets of summer
by saucers of skimmings spooned on bread,
never sliced, always folded into a wedge

of layered comfort offering up the bleed
of its sticky filling, to drip down my chin
to wrap my soul in its fragrant kiss.
And her neat aproned glow with a voice
sweeter than the confection spooned
with a hug that surpassed berries by the ton,
and any jam sandwich folded then, or since
Even the one by my side now. It's not the same.
I'll put it out for the ants swimming by.

The Cast

He could've been a thousand years old. Fisherman
solid in his stance, oblivious to the swirl of wind
around his billowing legs, not in waders as maybe
I expected wandering past in the scuff of a sprouting day.
In his hands, the lazy arc of an invisible line defined
only by his motion praying towards the waves
and the muffled plonk of weight and hook rippling
the surface before the unwelcome prize, unseen
glistened to the settle of sands below, waiting.

It all came back to me in this worship to the sea.
That salty glint of a tear in one eye, listening
to my father curse the Gods, who had knotted
his line with only a small boy to check his words.
I can feel the gentle tug now, tucking me safely
into the bend of his stance, the nudge of effort
and the fading plonk, like the muffled strike
on a fading memory, settling in the sands below.
I can never remember if the prize was claimed.

Sewing Petals on to Poppies

what do we need from days?

too busy with their own plans
too busy to notice your fear of solid ground
too busy to catch your stumble when you trip
on the jut of sun cut into the dark alleyway
of an unexpected consequence

what do they expect from you?

to sense the space that reaches out
to catch the hush in a caring hand

every day this week I've walked past a rubble bound clump of
red poppies, paper thin, fading in the mixture of grub and sun
under the rumbling concrete dripping the rush hour bleed
what do they expect from me?

I knew they would die, smothered not by my thoughts
nor by my words, their petals gone, leaving tombstones
of brief memory missed by the rush of thoughts and words
passing daily, oblivious to their death floating past
not uncaring but busy planning their own wilt

to sense the space that reaches out
to catch the hush in a caring hand

what do you want from me?

when the itch of my existence bone deep in the caress of your
thoughts

when the words I shape are not important, when all I want from me
from them, from you is to catch the pause before the wilt

beyond the rush of strangers passing to hold what remains of us
in the space between my words and to settle there with me

sewing petals on to poppies

The Estuary 1914

Mud flats: beginnings of shifting lands
Spring tides and the promise of kisses
Lost in shallows, like elvers weaving
Uncertain of the compass points

Assassin stalks: days moving ancient bones
Distracting the break of honest toil
Upwards through buds and leaves and
Nests embroidered with inherited wisdom

Mud flats: uncertain journeys, tadpoles
Like mini submarines shimmy black
In the lift of silt and missions planned
In the un-timbered trenches of autumns past

Falling crowns: and pebbles, in the tumble
Of shallow waters hurrying to the estuary
Resolute knots of mussels inhaling cool
Through polished shells of shimmered blue

Mud flats: in the splat of engines starting
And men in waders hauling the nets closer
The mesh of ropes and floats, and silver
Bars of salmon lifted from the run of gravel beds

Distant thunder: brushing the lick of daft calves
Where the warmth of summer turns the air
Inwards and upwards to burst the clouds
Into rods of blood and fresh deliverance

Mud flats: in the cold lights of tarry sheds
Of seedlings softly teased between fingers
Then nursed into the damp kiss of earth
To strengthen limbs in quiet reflection

Armies gather: rumours of wood smoke
Chase the mocking response of sea gulls
To bleached limbs of scrawny youth piling
Bicycles, half suspended in the willow herb

Mud flats: where I gaze now and think
Of them in the random graves of innocence
Abandoned bicycles, the broken compass of
A generation and the kisses never collected

High tides overran the summer. Ghosts now, of
Bleached limbs crossing the mud flats, searching
For the wind heaved spot where they'd planned
The routes of unhurried journeys never to be taken

Terra Nullius

crimson red flowers, thousands
a spreading bleed of them
a hole in the rot of humanity
at odds with the bastard landscape
in which they flourish – *terra nullius*
the jarring sharp edged midden
of blistered tangle and rusted life that is not death
but hope abandoned
to exist in its own unravel of nothing
where to survive is to be invisible to those who cannot be seen
who exist and cultivate the till of cinder, dust and bones
the discard of mankind too busy
to notice the struggle of the weak
shaken to their core
by the rumble of Gods and Snobs passing by
sucking the juice from the earth
preening their way to the bridge
caring not a breath for the unseen
nothing but rubbish, poisonous and pointless
to be ignored by all the important pilgrims queued
to cross the rainbow tossing a penny
or a scrap until the dawn of horizons
when the path quietly, softly narrows
when the invisible become the visible
and the road to the bridge becomes the landscape
and the bridge becomes the rainbow, its foundations
bound to the stalks of millions of crimson red flowers
visible from all the corners
of the Nine Realms shining

Wisdom's Juice

Somewhere in folds of dreams, Vanaheim
Floats on boundaries of imagination; in time
To swallow heavens with magical disregard
For complexities born of human chaos

Banishing greed and fury to the grub of Utangard.
No need for pale weakness in shabby human form.
Through widening hollows in battered walls, a storm
Sparked by Odin's scheme, of vengeful desire
To suck wisdom's juice from blackened earth
The mulch of trampled souls lost in bloody mire.

Breathless rivers pooled, their exhausted course
Amongst the crumble of once proud walls; a source
Of peace, a reluctant path worn across the middle plains
By sated Gods; a deal planted in shifting, bartered sands
But memories itch, to bubble up amidst fractured stains.

The salted lick of revenge on Vanir wounds never far
In embroidered days of counselled grace, the precious star
Of Mimir's wisdom doomed to die in a severed blast,
Tossed in the saddle bag of bitter scorn at Odin's feet.
In his weeping embrace, nurtured, its spells yet to be cast.

Butter Beans and Lum Hats

My Grandad didn't like poppies.
He liked vegetables - butter beans
And cabbages - a sentry in a Lum Hat
Impassively staring across the allotment
- trenches of turnips waiting.

I'd watch him scythe through grass
And mutter in crumpled silence,
At the tissues of crimson red
Left dangling on the barbed wire
- withering before their time.

He didn't like poppies, or pigeons.
I'd watch him pluck and mutter
In the crumple - at the exposed flesh, blood
And white feathers floating easily across his mind
- whistling a lone piper's lament.

He didn't like poppies. He loved their roots
Buried under their innocent weight
Of the soil that nourished his soul.
I'd watch and listen to his silence
Marching across years to Verdun.

from

'THE RUBICON OF ASH'

Thrapple Douse

the mair Ah vote the thirstier Ah become
tae soothe ma thrapple and aye maun
see the Scotland o ma hert's desire
wi sperklin tides and independent fire

the mair Ah dream the thirstier Ah become
tae quench ma passion in freedom's sun
an settle stappit oan the skimmin saunds
wi ma pals fae yon supposed foreign launds

nae mair tug o war, or falsehood fears
fechtin ower a shrivelled thistle's tears
but tae treat it gently, like a precious gem
nurtured sweetly, and passed tae them

the bairns o oor tomorrows, incessant blaze
in their een, through which Ah contented gaze
oan a future, ane o guid times an success
whaur aabody is thocht o nothin less

nae matter whaur they marked a cross
tae douse their thrapple, nae fir a loss
o transient joy, wrapped in politics
but haun in haun in a befriended mix

ane voice o the fowks wha matter
thon band o grafters, ower the scatter
no left ahent by greed or poverty
but staunin prood o a nation's liberty

Spring Lifts

A day in rags, brittle dreams wake from sleep
like striking a rock of moss bound journeys.
It's a path, a future
of cherished plans folded into the soil.
It's a note of song that settles without expectation
on your shoulder, to change your face and steps.

I don't have a map. I don't know if one exists
of journey's planned but not yet travelled.
Those scribbles on a napkin, taken down
from a shelf, marked in the book of poetry
that you've read by the window all winter.
It's a path. The future slips from the page
and waits at your feet. Pick it up.

Decorate the Roof

decorate the roof softly
down to a space where
simplicity of thought thickens
with every drop of rain

where fat clouds unburden
and you're transfixed
by the hypnotic drum roll

of patterns pooling
of drops forming,
flowing

into fragments of ash
in poems unpicked
and breaths absolved
spilling like wine

until the drains bubble
and froth like sugar
on the heat
of the untended stove
and words stick to your eyes

forming poems of sweet futures
where the ash has no meaning
and the river passes no more

The Old Mountain Sleeper

Every morning, it fills my window
or at least, it fills my attention.
A wise bludgeon of mystery,
a cock-sure rub of its shoulders
above the mist, folding down Glen Isla.

A measured presence, all mathematical,
trigged, precise - watchful
in the slump of unplanned days,
like a pyramid at odds with the pines
columned, defending its bracken socks.

From here, Boy watches, counting pigeons
and Mrs Christie hangs out boiler suits.
Even distant rumbles of trucks on the by-pass
hoovering up the miles, seem unaware
and have muffled deeper into the distance.

I don't know if an ancient King sleeps
at its heart, waiting for a signal, sword
held tight in the gauntlets of my imagination
or if the signal is a distant light catching
polished granite slab at just the right moment

but every morning, I light the halogen beacons
in my bedroom and angle the window
to reflect the dream beams to chance
the awakening of a distant poetic mystery
deep in the soul of Mount Blair. I am Boy.

Rattling Cans

The only witnesses to him were the peeling tea roses
on the mill house walls. Their fading beauty blackened
by bitumen reek from the slow burn death of a railway sleeper,
a three-foot stub of its original strength.

His right foot nudging it a little more into the crumbled edge
of a fire barely lit, slumbering in the clamp of the one room,
in the one house still standing – his fortress, his last stand
alarmed and bound by a web of string and rattling cans and cats
patrolling the curved sooty edge of the fading sleeper glow.

They said he was a spy.
They said he was a boozer.
They said he was lost.

He was none of those. He didn't need to be found.
I could get as far as halfway up through the staircase web;
enough to rattle cans, leave him stuff, apples and bread, milk
for the cats.

He was an old soldier.
He didn't need to be found.
He'd done that himself.

I met him once more,
the day they knocked his home down.

He gave me a bundle;
of notes
of words
and treasures beyond me.
How I wish I'd kept them.

They put him in a Shelter.
He died the very next day.
He'd found a way out without rattling the cans.

I'd lost a bit of my way in.

So when cans are rattled under your nose
– think of peeling tea roses,
think of him.

Pushing Brake Lights

pushing brake lights into darkness
effortless, oblivious to the stress
keeping up the rhythm
set by the bus
three rows back on the left
always left
so you can see the pavement
the houses flickering into life
their doors opening, lives widening
into the throng of chaos
dampness, depression, schoolboys
guided by the lights of phones flickering
words of three syllables, I don't understand
like the first time I told the young woman
she was fit, catching the 7:56
schoolboys laughed so I wrote a poem
in the condensation of the window
unable to stop heat escaping from my face
I got off at the next stop
a full stop to the straight-backed search for solitude
and I watched my unfinished poem
being wiped away by the fit woman
nearly late for work
but she wore my poem
on her sleeve all day

The Heavy Sky

the sky is heavy with reluctance
tomorrow broods like a coiled snake
muscled, prepared to bite back
unaware of the fear it weaves

midwinter settles into the seat
with fresh batteries in the remote
and folds its arms in defiance
towards the arid desert of words

posers and pontificates counsel up
the shiny green seats, strutting and
time rolls on without a pause, into
a pavilion of bells and divided shadows

the renegade prison of conscience
adapted to take the strong spine, tolls
the peel of names, in the open veins
of Demos, and bleeds the roses dry

The Lost Trig of the Ninth

My friend Malky has been on a mission, for what seems a lifetime, to find a trig point somewhere on the Gask Ridge, west of Perth. He has never found it despite numerous cycling and walking expeditions. I have my own theory as to why:

Who is this coming along the road?
Cycling like Billy O, as if in the downhill
fury, leading the Tour off the highest col

knuckles white in the grip of enthusiasm
eyes streaming with the anticipation, and
unwavering where the worn path ends.

Who is this, not so much a leader, but an explorer
plotting his way towards glory through the briar
his Ordnance Survey in one hand folded under scrutiny

a flask of soup in the other, puzzled, perplexed
walking to where he thinks I stand
on top of a shaky Gask Ridge hummock

the slightest smudge of lines on the map
along the fence line, past alder and birch
at the far end where Alex the Orraman

snecked Jean fae the Post Office and now
the weighty ambitions of an explorer dust
the horizons with sweat from a shaken helmet

I am here. I have watched you seek me out
I am not a bare stone box, an upturned coffin
manufactured by some anonymous Ministry.

I am more than that. I am the sum of your itches.
I am tattie bogles and Wisps stuffed in a jar.
I am the Still of the last dram ever poured.

I am a stack of helmets bound with four shields
and the spears of the bravest centurions ever.
I am the Lost Trig of the Ninth

and into your virtual adventures I've passed
un-noticed, dropping rose hip seeds into your head
each grain engraved with another clue to finding me.

Laughing to myself, knowing in time you'll arrive
past the alder and birch, the smooching spot of lovers
coming and going, neither empty nor whole, absorbed

in the mystery but not at odds with your journey
simply lost in the contented glow of your efforts.
Your soul exceeding its circumstances with honour.

I am here, friend of the trig. We welcome your search.
Next time you seek me, leave a spear or a bicycle pump so
I can tell the Legions of your bravery, my Friend of the Ninth.

Slate

After Ballachulish

As you sat with me in silence
in the field of mouse eared hawk

I heard the industry of the quarry:
the rumble of the digger shaping it

the call of the gaffer, and the mason
counting out the marks of time

and lads moving the slate sheets
like gravestones on the standby list

for unplanned funerals, when far
reached journeys came home to rest.

The birthplace of roofs, now stacked
abandoned in rows, pushing heavy

against the whitewashed stipple
of the Ironmongers, in competition

with spinning rods, rainbows, beach balls
and the resentment of the curlew's plea

sadly calling, heavy, rain-soaked
all mud-slick in a smothering breeze.

I watched you walk towards the sea
and counted the hours lost between us.

The Cathedral Field

Walking the dog, at dusk in the cathedral field
is to occupy the same space bonded only by thin light.

As much as the company transforms your thoughts
his attention flits in and out like an angry wasp off the leash
occasionally buzzing your legs then flying off at an instant
into cloisters of young spruce, spooking the old pheasant
like the choirmaster defrocked in a compromise, his modesty
exposed in the blush of bronze on the lopped branch
before settling above the centre path.

The broken beech nut mulch softening our routine pace
in the imagined aisle in a field set up for a wedding.

To the left, the bride's family, birch, silvery white, practiced.
To the right, the groom's faithful, beech and cool silver sheen
with copper socks and the odd flash of sun kissed moss.
All waiting for the bride to appear when the last snows shift
gracefully from the shoulders of Ben Vorlich
transforming bare branches into vaulted jubilation
where the brilliance of light measures our time in birdsong.

A Single Feather

is all that remains:
tightly bound strands,
weaves of light and shade
soft gaps and loose knots
of memories before the loss.

The perfect distance walked
on familiar paths, through days
until, dropping his eyes there
it lay, un-fluttered. He stopped
and shared a weave of thoughts,

a skeleton of light and shade
on a random path, remembered
where they first met, drawn
to the shapeless, muffled hour
by a single feather, lifeless

but still pushing air through
the stifle of the flattened earth
resting beneath a flightless sky
until the wind shifts, soundless
with no detail on its edge but

enough to smudge the shade.
Now the clouds break, gaps
appear in the crumble and
the feather lifts in the cool air.
Strands open and knots loosen

new gaps stretch in the curve
where he finds space to breathe
until the wind settles, catches
in the snag of thorn stitched paths
and nails a feather to his feet.

A Full Hand O Bananas

The Pap is a two-banana climb,
    maybe with an added Caramel Wafer
        for the bonny view across Loch Leven.

Aye, there's Munro baggers, and Corbett tickers -
    I've bagged a few stotters, ticked a few beezers
        and they're never the same - always unique.

That's why we love them. They're like us - different
    but all fused to the hills we climb, sweat, dream
        and curse up in sun and rain - ignoring the midges.

Me? I'm more a big round lumpy sort of person.
    I've clung to a few jaggy ones, with my brother
        before yon chanty rasslers stole his bloody pech

and left him wi' yon MS thing, and besides, now
    my knees are 50% Lego and 100% peanut brittle
        and it's not the same without him, loosen me

somewhere, along the polished skite of a ridge
    on a full hand of bananas kind of mountain,
        being jogged passed by protein bars on legs.

So here I am, on the Pap, reminiscing
    on the rock where we toasted his Big Four O,
        eating my second banana, with no-one to share the view.

I'll save my Caramel Wafer
    for the drive home up the Glen. I'll smile
        and respectfully nod to my right - three banana sisters

in a row, and a ridge of six bananas to my left,
    before the majesty of the Buachaille's, the moody
        four bananas of the Beag, the extra wafer of the Mor

and the luminous folk on the Crowberry Ridge,
    knotted together in their four-wheel drive ballet shoes.
        I crazy love them because they're just pure bananas!

Revelled Thrums

yon skoddy notion o daein summit, ill-best,
gaun tae War until yon Pointless Celebrity Jungle Factor
distracts wir confeesed-like state o breathin

no mindin sanitised deid, random
laser-precise deid, blastin ticks-in-boxes deid,
collateral daith-hampers contained in easy-tae-swally deid

no mindin media-friendly, manipulated, runkled auld deid
drizzled ower the confection o wir normality deid, then
pre-recorded intae the glitterati pokes o pourit tributes

as lang as yon daith-ruckle, yon eftershock, the rave
disna tak up prime time, or ream-fu yer Sky Planner
wi barrel bombs an corpies blank gawpin

else no oan the new carpet, or the chairs wi bocht
in thon Farm Roup – braw bargains rocht fae deid - when life
wisna cheap but somehow noo it is – that's the state o it

yet death-yirm, muffled in the trimmed settle o conscience
we leave lyin oan mortal slabs, forlayin, sklims ower easy
through the blistered grille o wir false confessionals,
        tae ham-shackle us

an chaingin channels willna save ye fae the Deil Maister
fir him, wha cares nuthin o the pleasantries o mourned daith
comes wi his ain remote control, an aa Eternit tae find yer
        Favourites

Hutton's Bones

Iridescent camouflage. Once Summer light finds
the correct angle, it settles and I find the altar.
I stand alone in the cool sharp shadow, studying

touching the edge of basalt, polished blue, wise
to the soul-free tourists of ordered years -
a passing of truths in the knowledge-breeze.

Hutton, his words pulled free from the Crags,
nothing significant, everything uncertain,
merely knew of truths in the grain of journeys.
Unrooted wisdom, relocated by the hammer knock,

and a delivery of sensation into new language,
to purify gazing out across Reekie, blinking

until the scholars, and the seasoned pious
by their acclamation of his understanding
offered his bones up to the throne of Arthur.

The Rubicon of Ash

We will lean on the clouds once too often. Perhaps
on a day fed up of whispers, where the wind holds
the camphor scent of quiet reflection as it snaps
the polished floor with the voices of our pasts.

We will become centurions of awareness, encrusted
with jewels, dragging the swollen coffers of our journey,
but trapped on the wrong side of the Rubicon, like a frost
of sweet anger, and a thousand nights of passions lost.

We shall never reach the gates where the piper plays
in the roofless tower with only ravens to mark time
on his lament, leaving us to roam the river's edge by day
in search for a crossing point, and lost in shallows by night.

And when I try to scream, soft ash falls from my lips
leaving only cindered flakes of my salvation, where
the water laps my naked body and mocks my shadow
as the piper's call fades through the rushes of sorrow.

It used to be Bottles

It used to be something, once in a while
to read of a bottle washed up on a beach
with a scatter of words cast on another tide
saying hello from a dot on an old school map.

Sometimes, it would make the newspaper,
in the local section between a notable death
and a prize for jam or the odd photograph
of the potato that looked like your Granny.

It used to be bottles, now it is drifting shoes.
Sometimes, they will make the newspaper
but mostly they don't because we'd rather
read about bottles and words from dots.

There are too many shoes, but none with words.
Their message is more subtle, imprinted
in the insole, like the rings of the felled pine,
counting outwards the life now surrendered.

Sometimes the message in the shoe is hidden,
covered by the wrinkled foot of the drowned
on another tide, on an old school map, a dot
shaded in pink where the Empire screwed us all.

It makes the newspaper, just another death,
not so much notable but just as a passing dot
until another odd shaped vegetable surfaces.
Oh, how we laugh and forget the insoles of the felled.

The Gouge

storms care nothing
for memories of walks
and will gnaw and gouge
the steady embankment

willing the tree to fall
achingly to its knees
re-arranging the curve
of the river's ambitions

you can shout at the rain
and touch the bark of
the wounded but only
the birds know its pain

The Fixed Jury

Rowan slump. An acceptance in the smoke.
Smouldering layers in the crackled step.
Dispersing memories, upwards, upwards.

Slash and burn. Impatience over reluctance.
The time to mourn lost on the first match strike.
Prayers for the living held back in daffodil bulbs.

But the magpie counts the spirals, cackling
when the snap of branch surrenders its soul
to the soft, gauntlet grip of the quickened feast.

A banquet of supple death, plate-less, forked
through the mulch by the diners, in bent toil
gorging on the hollow sound of winter's blessing.

Blackthorn quiver. A fate smeared in orange paint.
Trial by fastened eye where the ditch rim slab ends.
Genocide folds across the barn top and drowns.

The pitch of salvation in the songbird's thrapple
Doused by the engineered choke of the cunning
And the scavenger's menu of managed tyranny.

In Melody

This morning the birds
        stopped
   silent
but I knew they were there
   shallow breaths
waiting for attention, and gifts.

A grey smudge
       and matchstick sun
    muffling song
pressing chests, queued in layers.

Breathing is
      an assumption
of our own unpicking: willingly
writing down the hours. Death
but a sweet, gentle conclusion.

Sing your hours.

And feed the choir in melody.

The Bicycle
After Paris 2015

Padlocked. Black. Unsure like the Paris sky,
abandoned in the enforced sobriety of chaos,
a bicycle supports the weight of a single rose,
petal after petal wilting, never to be held.

Its owner, dead among the dimming café lights
between the vastness of huddled innocence
and the visible spectre of cowards. Haunted.
Not broken. Not surrendered. Re-assembled.

The helicopters shadowing, counting, reporting
how they re-appeared in their thousands, nervous,
defiant, to reclaim the streets, to reset the tables.
A single rose on a table for two lovers. Unlocked.

Plainsong for Murphy

yon spuggies dinnae seem ower quarrelsome the day
in a jaggy bush o holly burstin wi polished abundance

tho yon rain micht hae scunnered their grumpy itchiness
nae so agitated and permittin sun's tendrils tae cosy

the spindly legs o fluffy pesterins, until Murphy appears
workin' a lather in and oot the dip and steal o hedgerows

there wis aince a time when wee yappin dugs nipped
ma heid, but nooadays Ah'm comforted by his plainsong

in choirstalls of emptied birch linin yon path, smoked
through the cloistered solace of oor plentiful wanderins

and whaur him and Ah hae conversations o national importance;
the speed o pigeons, biscuits or carrots, single grain or single malt

then a cackin pheasant bursts oot the forage derailin
oor train o thocht an plainsong becomes aa jangly in pursuit

o the grain robber, and wi a the devotion o a causeless rebel
only to be saved by offerins o carrot shaped sacraments.

Innerpeffray

On the time served bench, a soft withdrawal,
engrained reflection inhaled with birdsong.
Nothing prevails beyond the winds brisk enquiry
and pressed thoughts gathered in my pocket.
Behind me, ordered words. No age or sign,
only knowledge sentried in the pine-board settle.
On slabs, in rafters and steps, old whispers
of counted diction. Learned and squared off
behind its whitewashed and cherished register.

How long the field has shaped across the river
and is measured in the precise, spring drills
by generations, stoop-set, measured, still digging,
still interested, perhaps unaware of the books
beyond the planting, perhaps born from soil,
cultivated, nourished to be of the words,
layered above the bend in the river, where
the shifting effort of water lifts its story
into the settled ken of Innerpeffray.

Old is Tomorrow
The words in italics are the last four lines from Hugh Miller's book, My Schools and Schoolmasters.

You can see it clearly, if you allow yourself, to pause, to
        breathe out
for the briefest of moments away from the grub
that befuddles our imagination, the digital bleed of information.

life itself is a school
and Nature
always a fresh study

layers of past generations
mulch of past millenniums
the openings, the chasms
the marks of ancient furrows

successive soils laid bare in stratified gravel, moraines of
        memory unpicked
by him, to be scooped up, understood - learning
the memorial of time, a clock ticking past
our fragile existence barely
a thin layer of history visible, relevant – brushed
by the frequent eddy of tides where humanity shifted along the shore
and in that shallow glimpse of our past, man
emptied his mouth of gravel and found the plough to till his story

and that the man
who keeps his eyes
and his mind open
will always find fitting

How long have we stumbled and understood nothing? Not him.
He walked with a steady pace: noticed the difference,
even a section of a few feet, our two lines of pointless text
        message lost
where in that time, he would find an archipelago
of islands, brushed by frequent icebergs, and the lift of creatures
sub-arctic molluscs, sand floods, a belief
in all that's left under our feet, belongs in our minds, in our
        imaginations

though it may be
hard school masters
to speed him
on his lifelong education

I am sure of this – Hugh Miller's stride was unbroken, in seeing
        our story.
His footprints apparent today in the unravelling
of our tomorrows, the unfurling coil of our layers, the unlocking
        of ourselves
to place fresh words on the shelf next to his

Siller Sooth

Tidins o seasons stappit fou o fechtin spirit
Spitin water thrawn ower their bricht endeavours
Tae sooth oor kittle days wi tunes o golden merit
Rocht wi chitters, hunkered doon wi drookit feathers.

Ane whiles they chirp an chap the mossy bark
O siller birks, an holly circlin the childless days,
We ignore their joyfu ballads wi oor fizzled spark
An a perilous trait o bendin mither natur's ways.

Yon global warmin pokin the swell o the bourgeoisie
Layerin the fat wi blindin greed tae toast wi' glee
The burnin branch o the last o the mahogany
Ain o the sharpest truths whiles we aa drap an' dee

Let the lichtie show up ma wirds, afore it's ower late
Whiles the warnin's in their song, fearfu notes o truth
Fugged in oor lugs o ignorance. The comfiest state
O oor wealthy pairts, no sensin yon endless sooth.

We need a michty shak fae oor contented wander
Afore the birds depart and the sangbuik floats away
Oan tides o forests, drooned by oor muckle squander.
Whit is oor worth if we dinnae seize this opportunity?

from

'MIND THE TIME'

and the

ST JOHNSTONE F.C. RESIDENCY

Open the Curtains

open the curtains, inhale the birdsong
it's Game Day,
Saturdays have always been fitba' days
we've had a break, a summer break
doing stuff, being buried to your neck
on the beach, by the bairns
on the Mastercard, by the other half
but here it comes again,
you can sense it, scratching, itching
bubbling up at the back of your eyes
folded into the plastic sleeve,
next to your season ticket
tucked behind the clock,
puzzled by your lack of attention
hidden behind the list for the Big Shop,
which will need to wait until Sunday
because Saturdays are fitba days
but wait, there's live games on Sunday telly
and Monday Night Football, then
Champions League on Tuesday, Wednesday,
UEFA Thursday the last 16's on and on
and oh, aye the Friday night game
but there's always Click and Collect
because Saturday's are fitba days
and anyway the Take Away does home delivery
or maybe something out the freezer
until after the winter break, before the split
because well, you know
what I think about Saturdays

Unner the Fold

**Andrew Watson was the first black professional footballer.
He played for Queen's Park and Scotland before moving to
England. A remarkable man.**

in the sports section, twa paragraphs
unner the fold, an oot o the spotlicht,
Ah saw a photograph o a toosled chiel
impassive, beckonin me tae find him
beyond the January transfer windae

proodly displayin his country's badge
oan a jersey o pink an' yellow bands,
no in a puffed oot boastin way, no
in a hunkered doon ashamed way,
but as it shid be, ane o his nation's best

a nippy ain tae, wi a hint o Jinky's weave
awready capped fir Scotland, his faither
a sugar plantation owner, a player o sorts
but as Ah listen tae the kettle bile an coffee
steams the inky stains oot ma thochts

Andrew Watson's gaze turns aa sombre like
when he hears the Classifieds, his noble
Queen's Park no daein sae weel nooadays, no
since he went sooth, gaun fae tanner ba enigma
tae bein swelled up in time added oan.

Turnstiles

Dull, ageless cranks and oily turns. A cold steel
push, anti-clockwise in anticipation, expectation
every time but different then, off Florence Place
off Dunkeld Road, in cold skies, and bright days.
The bustling blues in ear shot of Muirton aces.

A bustling Asda's now. Terraces of sell by dates
pitch views hindered by pristine aisles, walls
of soups, cereals and bargains to be netted.
There, the turnstile my dad showed me, the gate to
being grown up, following him, to follow the Saints.

In through a gap. A cupboard door. A secret passage
blistered blue, a Tardis stripped bare to a briar of steel.
A soft putty face waiting, trapped in full moon cheer.
The murmur of passwords, an exchange of promises.
Me, squeezed close into legs, the big lift into a contraption.

A time machine whirring into action, releasing me,
into a new world, the land of my future dreams,
heartaches, and glories sunk into a bottomless heart.
To be trailed for years, through cupboard doors, images
on a loop, seasons lost in the sunlit absence of him

handing down the password so when the crank
and turns of a McDiarmid Tardis pulls my son with me
into the briar tangle, the turnstile lifts our respect
towards the rows, of my Dad, sitting with your memories
and in front, Willie Ormond with Drew Rutherford

up in the corner, amongst a throng of ageless Saints
on a wooden bench, white squared and numbered.
The perfect view brought from the old ground, loyalty
stitched in to the respectful wave of unfurled scarves.
Their souls steadfast in the crank of the turnstile forever.

Rituals

Wear the same scarf again
and the same jersey again.
Expose your heart again
on the same sleeve -
again because rituals matter.

They matter - bottom six,
top six, last man standing,
beating the drop,
reaching the top – sliding
uncontrollably downwards
but acknowledge the effort – always.

Use the same turnstile again
the same queue again
for a pie, you'll eat again
crust first, then the lid
again because rituals matter.

They matter – in Europe
or maybe not, or stop the rot
bottom six, never top six -
last man standing
in the glare of live TV
or on bended knee, praying.

Fear the future again,
grasp the chance, the
through fingers glance,
practise your scream
but, and never forget

if your neighbour stumbles
in step, in word
in remembering, hold out a hand
help them up
because rituals matter
always.

Non-Season Blues

Early June, and at odds with the day.
There's a JCB digging at the Ormond end
scraping the red ash back, exposing sores:
the missed chances, the soft goals aching
and the Celtic defence where it was buried
by themselves, before they headed home.

It's beyond post-season.
It's not pre-season.
It's non-season yet it's busy, industry
swarms around the ground, puddles
into laughter and a single voice calling
the play - the demand to stay off the grass.

Sparkies cherry pick the lights, bouncing
but not in Unity, and adverts come and go.
I breathe in the sweet air off the grass
and watch the shadows of gulls replay
random moves of a season still echoing
in the ranks of seats, blue, red - waiting.

I can hear the grass breathing,
roots of memory gently disturbed:
shoots of anticipation and ambition swell
under the sun's lazy impress on the pitch.
A shadow curves out for a throw
opposite the eighteen-yard line, unmarked.

No goals. No nets but the spots
where the poacher tapped in
where the legend rescued, lifted us
where the new lad found the line
where the big man found his curve
where the Gaffer and the Bairn stood firm - still there.

Each one seeded with a loyal purpose
in the soil, the shine of grass, and ourselves
so we can return to the dream, quenched
with fresh hope, and unplanned mysteries.
A whistling burst of Oystercatcher blows
full-time. I pick up the shadow. I'm ready.

The Big Shop

When the team ran out for the first time
I could have sworn I still smelled
my last Bovril as I shuffled into my seat.
This was it. This was The One,
the season where breathing would make sense.

When the Ref blew full-time
on the last day, we were emptied of purpose,
gum-chew freshers of Saturday's frippery,
the rituals of Big Shop, Colour Charts
and quality time with the family.

We became hollowed out, skin-toned bollards
stiffened and set in the ground outside Markies,
to be ridiculed, pilloried by non-believers,
precisely balanced, weighed down with bags
for life, with no game plan – death by a thousand bargains.

We became caricatures of our terraced ghosts,
gut-knotted spectres feeling for the off switch
to reduce summer's drag, flailing, plunging
into unwanted routines, ticking chores off the List
between pickings of slow death Euros, and far-off Copas.

When the team ran out for the first time again
we knew them, recited their names, familiar and new
as we wolfed down the pies and the anticipation
loosened from our shackled domesticity:
the chasuble, the cloth of prayers binding again.

At full-time, in the chill of reality, we pretended
not to hear the tannoy confess the score,
the promise we'd made outside Markies
in the rain, doubting next season, this season,
why this would be The One – the resurrection.

My head was burst, I was oblivious, confused,
a contented rut-dweller, a tumble of opinions
towards the Pub, cursing, judging, confessing,
never going back until the tannoy would call again
and somewhere, another chore is added to your List.

Perfect

some games, like tonight
  seem to creep up
tap you on the shoulder
distract you long enough
    to plant a memory
      in your head
to germinate, grow then
  settle quietly until a slump
      in a traffic jam
      a long flight
or reflected in the dew drop
  gathering speed down
    the coolest pint of lager
ever poured
  and you smile
    pick up the glass, the memory
like a rush of cool air
  then you're delaying the whole world
from moving on until
you've finished smiling

waiting on the next game can be perfect

One More Trip

keep one, desire one, breathe one more
a bracelet of events, a chain of circumstance
of tokens, darning needles of sun thread memories

flight tickets, via Brussels, Nice and City
beer mats, unpicked and engraved
with odd numbers, names and broken promises

match tickets, lost bar codes, and room keys
demagnetised by long seasons passing
and by the exhale of desire wanting more

untrusting, I stare and you flirt with me
I seek your confidence, urge your rhythm
that nirvana in blue and I sense your all

that is visible, clear and bright - that is
louder and noiseless and wrapped tight
in the body of all of us, and will burst up

out of all of us, to conquer doubting minds
then I'll fold my tartan scarf neatly for Vilnius
to keep one, desire one, breathe one more

Trust

In Atholl Henderson

The busy signals only coaches make with wise hands,
their crisp, loud whistles snapping off the empty stands -
cold fingers wrapped warmly around ribbon lanyards
setting ablaze fiery grins with prized Best Player cards.

Games were won or not, the holidays were fun - a lot.
All shapes, sizes - all budding Saints - every one or not,
shimmies o dribblers, thumps o strikers a to be rehearsed
when happy bairns wi waiting Mums and Dads dispersed

with dreams o caps for Scotland - all by Atholl inspired.
He helped to nourish, stoked their passion, tho he never tired.
He, a foundation of trust in bright young rainbows sprung.
He, a champion o games won or not, on the first rung

of a thousand ladders, youth finding life-levels, skills respected.
Here now, memories are sparked, and frustrations deflected,
Here now, a new fire, nourished, a Community of Saints founded:
the buzz of all you good folk, harnessed, qualified, grounded

with ambition to embrace difference, and banish pointless hate
of those bitter cynics, to leave their misconceptions at the gate -
they're not required - fit only for blue bins every second Monday:
here, we walk the ball together, letting ageless bairns play.

So recycle your yesterdays, your thoughts of what's inclusion.
Unfurl tomorrow's rainbows to colour your welcome intrusion.
While football runs saintly blue through our City's veins,
they'll bleed dry, without your hold on future's guiding reigns.

And when they come chappin at St Johnstone's crested door,
sit them down, and take the time, explain the running score
to the scribblers wi chiselled notepads and spellcheck'd restraints
so they may tell anyone there is to tell this of us - *Trust in The Saints.*

So What is This Called?

The history of scunnered includes all of us
in our shades of team colours, joy, misery
& everything in between

Me, I stare into a glass, sharpen a pencil
stare some more & nothing happens.

I should be used to scunnered, such
that we share a season ticket
& know each other intimately.

I will now do an hour of mourning
for the missed chances
followed by an hour of hee-haw.
I will blame all known Gods.

I do it shamelessly, will feel good
because I've done it so many times.
then I will empty the glass in a oner,
feeling resolved although nothing ever is.

That's what you get for following your club.

I could've picked another team.
I could've picked another sport
but no I didn't and understand this result
was just another knee in the bollocks
from the back catalogue of lifelong purgatory
wrapped in a shiny film of temptation
taped down with false promise.

I listen to the radio and ignore the comments,
the social media posts, the tags, the feeds & smile.

There is something wrong with me
besides the scunnered so I fill the glass once more
& retrieve the season ticket from behind the telly.

The Gaffer's Land

Written to mark the award to St Johnstone manager Tommy Wright of 'Manager of the Year 2015/2016'.

You've found your place here, in between, at the edge.
Palpable reverence. The players, the crowds busy
re-arranging your plans set before, confident
on the calm surface of your judgement, exposed
every time, scrutinised, dis-assembled in the efforts
of the quick and constant, the random, clean chaos
played out on turf before you - analysed, agreed
sometimes disagreed in the boxed seats behind you.

If fate called your name, you found your place
in this white bordered zone, this no man's land.
Something was set right in the unravelled plans
of he who went before, and the spotlight turned.

I've stood in your place, at the edge, in between
kicked every ball in an empty dream. Full of belief
I've inhaled the same air but there for sure, parched
an unbending truth exposed me. I was an imposter.
I nodded to the four corners, squared off and holy
smiled softly and returned up the tunnel grateful
away from the Gaffer's Land - your place set true
in the hearts and minds of us, your fellow travellers.

NEW POEMS

Flipstones

On the sleep tide of the myrtle moon
our promised stars dissolve away.
In the infinite, a dull bright forever
watching wilderness dreams splay.

On the sleep tide of the myrtle moon
heavy clouds unclip their jealous soak
and I become stranded, softly praying
for an eclipse to loosen its muffled choke.
The cool shade where the merle hush

eats into your absence, salted tender
into the antler spikes of cold quicksilver
on the only sea to which you must surrender.

On the sleep tide of the myrtle moon
I'm left carrying nothing but these,
a million thirsts of flipstones lifting
fresh words into pockets hoping to please.

Preen

Their precious gift of life shattered
by insanity through the narrow gaze
of cowards' eyes, bleeding ignorance blue

whilst the generals and the clowns preen
their egos in the froth of tragic ambitions
with words I believe will never stand true.

Amidst the haunted wrecks of religions
washed up on the beach, they impose
the hollow songs of old beginnings anew.

                              Yet still we queue for more.

Broken

Once the day has gone the way of others
and brushwood cinders match the sky,
we can call on the lost, our river brothers
to gather nets and watch the ripples die.

Once the canvas blanks the weakening light
and the wilting rose rejects the pointless thorn,
we can bleach the rainbows mortuary white
and eat stellar crusts until our time is born.

Once all the rivers run backwards, to slow
and treacle soft, in to pools of liquid sleep,
we can stop to think of what we know
to heal Earth's wounds from bleeding deep.

Beneath the Glass
For the Man of Atholl

You don't know it or maybe care
but you're a celebrity unearthed,
recorded in a digital and alien world
laid out for scrutiny, telling you
what you already know -
how you lived
how you died

Your honest grafter's face imagined
not uncaring or with malice but flat-lined
beyond yourself and your kent-fowk of Atholl
tilling heavy soil, getting by, not knowing
other plans for you, after you brought in
the last harvest, hugged your bairns
for the very last time.

Did you have bairns? Those gentle voices
who missed you at their next hushie-ba,
at the next bite of snow, your memory
caught in the stick reek mizzle, warm coils
of your absence, and the years drifting by.

But I want you to live a wee bit more,
just long enough to understand you,
to accept why you were disturbed for us,
to accept us and our need to embrace you
and to understand ourselves a wee bit more.

Change

We stopped at red where the falling
leaves unsettle their purpose,
rust signalling change in our journey.

On the amber the rush, the breeze
lifts, refuses their surrender –
urges them to go home, to wait

but the lock's been changed
on the green, on the branch
where unborn sleep, unaware.

Feathers

I think too much – the world and everything.
Children in Camps but in this world,
bombed in sun, abandoned in rain

bargained in closed minds. You surrender
to the pull on the leash, to catch the bus
before the first world leaves without you.

Where was the junction, the crease,
the smudge on the map where we split
and forgot our shared wanderings?

Speak up anyone who doesn't slump
under the weight of unravelling visions.
I can't hear you. Your mouth is full of feathers.

The Paper Bones

too slow
too stiff

too limbed
too human

landlocked, not
free to fly

skin intruders
bone gatherers
feather maskers

humans with faces
masking the skull spikes of
inquisition

bones of hazel, bound
with sinew and blood
running through air,
roots catching breath

tripping up intruders
mistrusting their urgency
to become bird

too human
too broken

we are arrogant
we know nothing

our terror of everything
poisoning every place
aching in one place
alone we die
alone, never to fly

folding, folding, folding,
paper bones again, again
trapped in cellars, not to fly
bending, bending, breaking
feather bones again, again

we are not good at accepting
we are not good at living
we are not good at understanding
we never will be

but all we want to do is fold
into the sky
bend
into the bark
break
into the earth

all we want to do is fly

be quick, be loose
be human
and fly

too free
too alive, to die

Theft

In memory of too many young souls lost to the Tay.

How can we complain
when the tide turns up on time?

It fills the muddy shoulders,
empties the city's choke – efficient

cleansing, until it steals innocence
and leaves a silted imprint

in the hearts of others.
One day at a time. Like the tide.

Whispers

In cool whispers
    midnight heralds
        and empty silence
            ripples past
   whilst the vespers
     of a huddled owl
       announce
          the turning hours.

Diamond eyed watchmen
   in velvet cloaks guard
     our exposed souls from

       the plagued ambitions
         of our inner darkness

until daylight unfolds once more.

Truce

The morning truce
of conditional solitude;
firelight resuscitating
weather-less hours
where I sit neither alive
nor surrendered.

Like a book,
no longer requiring
a bookmark to find the page,
this day falls open
to words, well thumbed
by the amnesty of birdsong.

Carpow

It bludgeons out of ordered space,
punches you in the head. Bulk thrusts,
bold jabs, ancient oars plough the gallery.

But tell me this, my fine Carpow boat -
since the tide fell away, sunk you in mud
what does your dead wood mean to me?

What life remains hidden in every gnarl
or in the uncarved space, half polished
and thumbed between stern and stern?

I stand in your path. Your navigation drifting
to half-lit sea roads. The oars-folk lift me
to where I can be of river, of now.

And I learn from your muscled curves
without deflecting from rippled journeys
we both now share - days to be explored.

But Carpow has strength in its silence,
in its engrained truths where it holds firm.
It remains of river, yet forever in solid air.

The Donald

Warm clay in the cool slip
    for the shaping of journeys.

The sun drowns in the fissure.

        He shapes, shifts
        and thinks himself as Creator,
        Omnipotent,

        but through himself
        he spits fear.
        He is Paradox.

He knows but what the stone weighs:

    the creation of destruction
    born from his unpicked words

    sand becoming grit
    and ice in their delivery

    of tortured falsehoods
    pinned to his lips.

The tide turns within itself, and the shore holds the moon close.

Perthicity

Ah'm okay wi it - yon culture stuff.
Ah'm comfy wi the idea ma City has it,
aiblins disnae ken it sae guid,
could dae better at tellin it,
embracin the difference in us aa
- yon brilliant gems o Perthicity.

Wiv been fou o culture fer ages
so Ah'm okay tellin the world a ticky mair
wi a shiny badge ower ma hert
tae welcome aabody tae oor cityscape
tae ingest oor vision o Perth.

And stranger-freend, whit if ye fa in luve
wi oor cultur, wi Perth, wi us gems?
And in time ah ken ye will.

It'll happen dram-sweet or brash-bricht
until ye bide or leave reluctant-wairm
but wi yer memory fu tae the gunnels
o us aa – yon brilliant gems o Perthicity.

Hamish

For Hamish Henderson

Ma pace gaithered whaur the seasons gaithered
wi purpose an wi the bracken beggin me tae bide.
Ah'd nae destination tho a fierce ee oan the first o mony neu horizons.

Ma journey wid tak me faur awa fae Ben Gulabin's dawchy neb,
past the auld Kirk's Haillie wirds – whaur every Amen
wis a beginnin fir the next prayer seepin oot fae kent herts.

Ah left hame uncertain but comforted wi ye aa in ma pocket,
wrapped in the lichen scrape fae the kissin stane o the gate
whaur the Shee rummles doon, whisperin mossy screivit vows.

Then a thoosan leaves exploded fae the path like puddy-doos
unfoldin in the coontless days o ma uncertain traivels
through the cotter gate whaur ah paused an thocht -

Ae sigh in the feltie's pain. Will ye aa traivel wi me?
Will ye no risk the comin rain? Ye'll cry nae mair.
This ma vow.

Ah've ne'er fund the tippin point whaur sadness stoaps at the
threshold:
the door jamb that haufs oor lives 'tween the shaidie o nippit pasts
an journeys yet tae be unraivelled, maybe ah never will but ah ken

when ma imagination felt the grip o this ancient laund an ah inhaled
its hunger so tae consume the sky an paint it aa the colours o humanity
an richt there, ma hauf-sarkit hert kent this wis ma destination.

Ah pit ma hand in ma pocket. Ye wir aa still there. Ah heaved ma bag
surely intae the rhythm o ma gait an ma journey in life began
whaur Strathmore unfolded its airms an lifted me up aa worldly

an ah heard the door close saftly in the jamb, fair pit-mirked
yet leavin a ticky licht tae lead me safely hame again
tae whaur the kissin stane still hauds ma thochts dear -

Ae sigh in the feltie's pain. Will ye aa bide wi me?
Will ye no risk the comin rain? Ye'll cry nae mair.
This ma vow.

Hunkert Doon

oan the platty, a sanctuary o sorts
up thon muckle dune we ca'd Snell's Hill
whaur fowk noo spile oor holidays
wi yon boot- camp pechin gowkiness
in their stretchy peerie-breeks

ah watched the machars sook in the tide
an the sand surrender its hurdies
an the osprey fecht the tewhits fir its supper
an the weans merriment threadin thin
an a burnt log, post-sassidge sizzle
noo slumpit, casten-awa

midst a saft drift o yesterday's mindins
stitchin their shaidies tae the brekwatter
afore foldin unner the hypocrip's gaze -
thon glowerin Mannie abuin Golspie
still seekin his stool o repentance yet

an ah sat an suppit the slae-berry brose
o a skurryvaig puzzlin ower a blank page
wi a mind shairp, yet a pencil shairper
an ah kent it then an ah ken it noo -

ah wis a thoosant year auld, primed
wi a thoosant year ahead o me
but richt noo, here on Embo beach
the warld wis lichtsome in ma haun
yet fou tae the gunnels o ma hert

an whiles the black-heids didna ken it
their skitterin cabal wis a comfort
tae me here oan ma perch, leefu-lane
fir aa the warld's thraw widna steal
ma dram sweet destination o thocht
hunkirt doon oan Snell's Hill.

Gunpowder Leap
For Frank To

if it only happened this once
if the leap you see
was only for this salmon
would it matter?

one endless journey
searing muscle memory
into the paper
with flecks of burn

where the water splash
explodes, reminds
you of the failure
of the first leap

you can be the salmon
you can always try again

you can change
the journey, the cause
and effect of the splash

accept the consequence
explode your dreams
through tomorrow's leap!

Pause

sea borne words, soft spoken syllables combining breath
from early light and the precise art of the tide turn,
the ancient rumbling beast which softly unpicks the grammar
surrendered by the horizon

here is where our innocence first collided
with the wave's rhythms over and over
repeating its verse and for the sea not to be heard
is to die - its song touches the back dunes, its words
leaving their influence on every unravel of the silver curve
and in that moment, a pause where it all makes sense

More Than Perthshire

You try to understand it and what happens?
It changes colour, re-shapes itself.
You stand back and take it in. Overwhelmed.

You take a brush to its canvas, a pen to its page
and on any day, the proffered hand
of kent folk, in about your day. Embraced.

I can sit with strangers and lift from my heart
the landscape of my home, and surrender
its beauty into accepting hands. Satisfied.

And I know, Perthshire will give all it has in return
when you love it - that dram-sweet love
of friendship, of neighbours and kindred spirits.

What If?

What if stars are only puncture marks
        in the overstretched canvas of night?

What if a scrunched up mind could be set free
        untying the knots in a hidden poem waiting?

What if each syllable holds a micro-plasm
        of your life, peeling away your future?

What if the moon has no dark side
        and teeters on the wall by a rusty nail?

What if shadows in the midday sun left a stain
        to mark the passing of our memory?

What if I said I loved you? There, it's done.
        I've confessed. There are no more *What Ifs*

Tak Tent
For Helen McCrorie, Comrie

The hills must have known it was coming, the bruising
of silt-waters and the open wounds of a tideless swell:
a flood of terrible images, of memories drained away
forever, leaving only dirt blood stains to mark its passing.
Then the slow unpick of belongings, decades of bonds
forced into minute adjustments, unsettled centuries
of histories churned out from kettle pools, pebble beds
redefined for the river to slow into once more, to find edges
willing on which to settle elbows without disturbing more time
and before Comrie's unplanned work began, a rebuild under
spotlights, community spirit linking arms to defend its own.

Farmers, sparkies, joiners, bairns, guid folks, honest grafters,
shovels and brushes, diggers, builders, cleaners of days lifting
the fabric of the village out of nature's midden, solid buildings
finding feet again, streets re-tracing their footprints again,
the flood-swell contempt cleared out of cherished ground soak
day by day to dissolve into air and leave fresh sprung futures
to bud out of the choke, drift into cloudless skies where sun
warmed bright endeavours, where neighbours shared echoes
of their past, to comfort each other in re-emerging dawns.
How do you fit your past in to a single suitcase? To escape the task
of deciding what's important - choosing sentiment over objects.

Now where the library breathes new life, respects the past,
village eyes tak tent, resolutely questioning and archiving
how far they've come, agreeing where they want to be tomorrow.
A level of challenging curation has settled on Comrie's folk
against the backdrop of in-turned books and blank labels
framing the past's windows where the rain is welcome
to a point but no further than the flood mark on souls, no
further than the cover of a recipe book of five generations,
the blurred lines of a diary, precious words ink-fused blue
where memories remain secure in hearts braced steady
against the flow - and all manner of things shall they well.

Toned Genuflection

In movement, in genuflection of curved air
they remember the bodies of children,
closed eyes lit by notes of lost song

curved silent reflection
curve again -

into vaulted space, shadows dance across
trappings of failed religions, question
bleached impressions of icons - remnants
of a first forgiveness,
a last confession,
the second and last coming defined in

turned tone genuflection
turn again -

into the morning where ash road patterns
pass windmills brooding, like vacant crosses
on the Appian Way but they dance forward
through a sea of corn, centurion stalk-spears
threatening, questioning

where do you take your rhythms? which of you
is the leader? what truths do you hope to find?

The sun with all its power to gift life, deny days
or quicken death, blesses motion repeated
by the dancers, arouses the grain husk wind
to lift dust to camouflage their hearts.

Keepers of movement - be our futures,
remember us, embrace our past of

danced rhythmic inquisition
dance again -

at the rise of the moon to guide feet
on journeys deemed impossible in sun's glare
where rhythm must be light for footsteps,
in darkness to outline gestures, the fusion
of phosphorous and vaulted moon.

Dancers understand steps they choose,
know where paths will take them,
to where journeys demand breath, poise,
& silent space at its solemn velvet edge,
to where feet stop memories dissolving
one by one, eyes open, finding lost song,
turning our pasts, one by one
turn again dancers
& return to the path

for in tomorrow's trinity,
silent reflection,
tone genuflection,
rhythmic inquisition
will return in movement again

Denial Steps

Stitching impulses. Then passions transfix
on a hillside, and again in the workshop light
a naked glimpse shivers in the spun air.

So the unravelling affair may have begun;
single threads, and cotton shroud denial
slip into sleeves with buttons where lovers bond.

And after the measured dance, what then?
No embrace. No brilliance of sparks in between.
A blank stare out of cold eyes left weeping, alone.

And it's all a fabrication of life, is it not?
Merely a mirror of our own fragile truths.
So remember your steps. Your knowledge-rhythms.

Wisdom

So whit's next? Wir sat here diddlin,
    scrievin aneath the flichty paths

o sand martins weavin and Jumbo's arrowin
    tae whaur the maples grow, ower yon muckle dub.

When you first came aboot me, Ah wisnae sure why,
    an for a puckle miles, a kent ma mither wis richt

    Ye're better wi a guid plate o soup
    an a game o fitba wi yer pals

For yairds, she wis richt, then nuthin mair
    could be heard o her wisdom, muffled fir noo

in the lift o birk leaf, an the splash upstream
    tae whaur the haws submitted tae yer bustle

tae sit aside me, aw pechin an drookit but
    wi a leal-hertit deek as if to say, 'Isn't this braw?'

Me and you - Scriever an Spaniel - canny companions,
    lichtsome o wisdom's feeble touch - 'So, whit's next?'

Wilt

Ah kent it wis comin, yon mark-stane o the year
wi plenty o notice but the hint-end
haes snuffled oot o the blue meestery
o yon far polished nib.

A purple slattern fauldin in aboot scaddit days
nae sae blusterin mair gradual like wi furtife steps sae sleekit
we didnae notice shaddie's nippy haun.

Its glaur bullyin oor resolve tae overcome oor complacency
until we glowpit intae it, stumblin ower its path,
ignorin the snippit wairnin cut fae yon atterin wind
pummelin in fae nor'maist wi lang ships o steel-ribbit sna,
hulls surgin, draggin an pullin ahent in roustie rackles,
the bane-sair resurrections o winter's lang-negleckit ettles.

Sic an ill-duin business, wi spirals o raivel
lashit tae thair splootery decks, like minarets o ice
caa'in the days tae answer in the bouin moon.

Hae a swatch doon yon berry dreels, aa slappit
in the rainge o oor narrie memories,
fushionless noo an desertit tae thair fate by us
cooried aboot the beacons o simmer
smoulderin, bidin oor time, fearful, waitin
oan the mauchy kiss o the bleezin wilt.

Stepped Space

You left me with nothing to tell.
A glimpse of perceived sun-fire
tucked back into a deep pocket,

our pine needled familiarity
accepting the return of words
whispered under the wind.

No other thing can be so perfect,
although it is night and day
and I know the space widens more.

Dance Essence
For Illie

A.
Imagine
a dancing figure
made of breath
layered over tears
over motion, power
in the very essence
of life, each thin layer
precious yet
too fragile to separate
for fear of weakening
the whole, the dance.
Imagine.

B.
There are springs
of rivers where
what begins
becomes dance, where
what grows
matches rhythm.
Mountains, clouds
and tumbling rain
catch the beat and
subtle stretch of limb

to the mouth
of the open sea
visible from miles
where the dance first
ended the drought.

C.
Dance creates
space for itself
finds room to expand
to pull you in, free flow
clearing of inhibition,
making space for you
to interpret, take part
when the space fits
your rhythm – and
when life stops
that space should be left
blessed by your soul
ready for another's dance.

Not Enough Red Lights

When a pointless world blurs behind the glaur
of the day, smeared through the No. 1 window
less the kebab salad art of he who sat before
but there's a seat in a warm bus & outside
it could be anything it wants - what you want
is to get home, with no care for your day fading
but bare-faced traffic lights control your thoughts.

Most days your brain unravels the work-stress
tangle between Mill Street & the Hospital
& every night you have the same thought, remote
flicking off work, on to neutral & you not caring
but wondering 'what the Wards have on for tea?'
& by the Burghmuir lights when you're wondering -
'what the hell am I making for tea? praying for a red

regulated long enough to let the last customer's crap
file itself far enough back to be irrelevant, making space
to make sense of domestic bliss waiting impatiently,
up the gloomy hill, him being pointless watching Pointless
then the wonder of science sets up straight greens
& before you know it you're in a needle sweat panic
drumming down Letham Road, juggling thought bombs -

The freezer's empty. Pasta? Again! Is my pay in?
What's my PIN? Co-op or Curry? Driver! What's the hurry?
Slimming World's tonight! Oh Shite! The woman
behind me sounds like that last customer. Slow man!
She won't know me. Stay quiet. There's no point.
The whole bloody bus now sounds like the last customer.

There are not enough red lights.
There are not enough Wards, not enough Hospitals
with patients sitting down to a well drilled tea
& this is only Monday.

Last Orders

On the Tay, I heard the curlew take hurried flight.
Monks imposed silence under the vaulted sky
and muffled its alarm with prayers. Shadowed faces
implicated betrayal with carved out solemnity.

On the Inch, the greed-stained faithless stooped,
driving black beasts into the hollowed chills
between the tide nick and the shallow graves.
The sleet with red eyes turned blind the cowards.

Under charred oak splintered by the Deil's hoof,
I heard their betrayal approach in the clatter
and felt the air thicken around me and the dust
of my father's silt away forever under my bones.

A hammer and a traitor's sword heavy with intent
drained my life away, and everything in me burned,
became urgent, wanted to stand, not to yield but
to go naked of crown yet be neither foetal nor mortal.

But forgive the givers at this desecrated, tumbled edge
where unless the treacherous deed finds fresh voices,
I will wait until the crossing between you and I is secure.
I urge you then, reach down, earth-bound to take my hand.

Glide

One to one. I come from the house of the albatross
in love with the very essence of the white heron
whenever her assured glide caresses my mind.

I feel something sharp, like fear unravelling in veins
close enough to the surface to reveal my love
yet uncertain they will survive your intense scrutiny.

One into one. Then I fade to the quickening resolve
to keep the bind strong, the steering sweep bubbling
tides – for the waters of our destiny cannot out run them.

Butterfly Gallery
For Frank To

under the spotlight
a butterfly explodes
into the gallery, settles
on the wall
and again, every time
another person stands to wonder
and I walk back across the room
and I hold back the light

the butterfly explodes
in both light and shade
as sure as darkness burns memory.
Like a mountain slipping into the sea
on every sunset bleed
there is enough water to save the mountains
but not enough to save the butterflies
and my mind sears into me

BOOM! FLAME! BURN!

as the dead crow flaps on the fence
like a black flag, unfurled and exposed
the butterfly burns
before me again
and dies before me again
yet still it floats away free
leaving me in the room alone
to wonder, to wait

for the next butterfly and
people will stand once more
in the light and the butterfly
will return once more
to be burned again.

I hate how I will let it happen
just so I can watch it die to float away

Salt

On a salt wind shrivel, winter's rehearsed intrusion
wreathed with thyme and rowan berry glow
not of dark remembrance, sleeved on brittle snap
but of rubies, cut to the call of feathered snow.

And there am I, entranced but I am not forever.
And there you are, on a distant pearly watchtower
a thousand feet high, on the dream shift of sand
where the raven keeps count and will surely find your hour.

Making Space

And in the clear sky, the faintest hint
of parallel lines, autumn's manuscript
unfolding across a late summer day.

Circled days of adventures and celebrations
falling from the calendar, wandering
aimlessly about the desk, uncertain

where to go. To what should they cling to
in the faultless decline of sun's blessing?
So few days to find safety in a bowl

amongst tokens and vouchers for days out
unaware their expiry dates have doomed
their crumple to the flirtation of bonfires

stoked with the splintered fragments
of a garden ache-laden, falling from trees
unburdened across a late summer day.

Tell

Don't tell me of the storms
or the colour of our stolen words.

Remind me of the long walk
when we sang the Marseillaise.

Don't tell of the curtains never drawn
or our empty seats in the front row.

Remind me of our slow dance, sunlit
lemons, and the olive tree's wisdom

and we'll sit forever with our backs
to the broken fence watching

the tide search for our footprints
in the sands of this unfinished journey.

Choose

So much to learn
so much to lose

          knowing
          believing

all knowledge
all belief

        suspended in clouds

all within your reach.

It's up to you to catch the ripest rain when it falls.

Shore Road Coral

For Susie Johnston

this circle of circles, rusted
coral-reef, this weld of scrap
strengthened by its union

of cylinders bound, solid
in a rheumatic crouch
on a shore-road by low tide

unafraid of tomorrow, not
to decline like this world
discarded - worthless.

Or have I mistaken
its salvation for humiliation,
its reformation for mockery?

It is not only the shore tide,
on the bend by King James
or the barbed walls of Binn

wielding the power, she
gave it hers, for others
to embrace its resurrection.

I can read only the fresh air
it permits to dry its innards,
of dampened inquisition

and see it for what
it has become, tempered
by new hands, and eyes

which like me, see the world
around it with mistrust
and know it is safe

as steel coral reef to me, or
whatever it becomes
beyond shore-road and low tide

in the minds of others. I leave
this circle of circles,
strengthened by our brief union.

Pearls

Some sounds weep into empty ears through frosted air.
Words of despair, guttural and foreboding, voiceless

between giving and embracing but they must be believed.
I have no reason not to but every reason to lift them up

to pull them clear of his transient mire, one sound tied
like a dripping tap to the next: precious pearls, one word

after another until the source of their anguish stops
and his ambitions become voiceless, if only for a moment

but long enough for the flood of humanity, to wash clear
his false boundaries of hate, his geography of ignorance.

I press my hand to the screen, and offer my closest bond,
a simple touch of defiance passed silently across an ocean.

Crossroads

us at the crossroads, contemplating us
waiting, trying to spot our truths as they pass

then you breathe shallow and lapse deep
into its influence where it captures the wind

that whispered briar of abandoned visions
and still us, unwilling to snag the difficult truth

for fear it will not accept the cowardly conditions
we must impose on its paper thin existence -

above the fires and cools, the crimson deep wallow
draining away our frustrations, leaving only the break

of shifting sands, where I sit alone, waiting on us
my mouth blistered with the count of falsehoods

Dougie

One of the tallest trees in Scotland, a Douglas fir living in The Hermitage, a National Trust for Scotland owned wooded glen, which lies two miles west of Dunkeld, Perthshire, surrendered to the elements in January 2017.

All I know is this: you were there for me,
when it mattered, or when I didn't even bother
to acknowledge you on our pine needle strolls
in about your cousins on the easy side.

I know you were there for other folk
but that's okay. It wasn't really two-timing.
We'd made no commitment beyond
a cheery 'Aye Dougie' for that was your name

and a wee shimmer of branch on a good day
or a creak of your old frame on the days
the wind got in about your puggled bones,
unsettling your roots dipped in the Braan.

Aye Dougie, you were there for me, the day
we scattered my Dad's ashes upstream.
I only hope some kind buddy will do the same
for you, now you've reached the easy side.

Silver Alchemy
For Dave Hunt

slow down
to re-connect, to capture
not forever, for a moment
borrow to whisper your image
into the grains – see
what your mind will allow
embrace the space, the light & dark
then let it go, slowly
to connect, to re-capture
the next willing soul passing,
slowing down to imagine
their space again

Waver

Raindrops grabbing her shoulders
holding without cause
the echo of past dreams
        dripping
          cold
without the wisdom
    why trees bend low
        in the loosened wind
    tender stemmed
in their surrender
    of summer's burden
    struggle
to re-invent their purpose
       to recall their youth.

It's an August day,
one of many bundles
     of hours, gathering
     upstream in pools
     uncertain
       tumbling
        re-arranging
before the faithful commit
to the headlong rush
    into deep calm
whilst rebellious lovers drown in ecstatic foam
never tiring of life's sweet imperfections.
She wavers.

Bleed

I'm snagged by the dilemma of reality.
Stark horizons bleed into my pockets.

Must I love my fellow being
when they seem intent on destroying our precious earth?
This earth of us.

Give me the undemanding company of pine cones,
goose feathers and the polished forgiveness
of a virgin tide.

Must I love, if hate is not in my heart?

A skene goes by, working as one, beckoning
lifting my soul which burns sore
in the pierce of poisoned intrusions.

The world is dark-flat for now.
So I wait for rain, for air, to breathe,
to light the paths of unharnessed courage
that surely exists beyond today.

Griz an Cateran
For ABF The Soldiers' Charity

Raise your sights!

The mountains are awake, waiting, all belligerent,
arms folded tightly across their bracken chests.
They stare you down as if to say *C'mon then!*
Impress us! Let's see what you're all made of.

What is this vision of unplanned glories you offer to the Gods?
Word of your adventures has reached the Caterans
and Cam Ruadh relishes the bounty, the pickings
of luminous clad explorers who stray from their folly.

The snow riven burns of winter, expose raw flesh
of granite and of polished skin, blistered blue and
bleak through the peat bog knit, unravelling slow
to be mistaken for tears of mocking enthusiasm.

The rustle of silver birch at first deafening
then lost amidst your efforts to breath, your
drum beat support mute in the deafening thud
of a befuddled heart pleading hard on your ribs.

Raise your sights!

because in the half lit grub the only voice you will hear
is your own in a sober whisper devoid of bravado snagged
on the branch where the crows will peck at your ambition
as if to say What were you thinking when you signed on?

Are you dreaming of a warm bed yet before Diarmid
reaches out from a gap in the thin, moss light where
his tomb elevates beyond the mizzle, to nod knowingly
and mark your passing by with a cold fingered cross

leading you to where the wind silvers your thoughts away
and fills the void with answers with no questions
like the grouse disturbed in a fusillade of wing snap
and its voice lands in your ears Go back Go back

Raise your sights!

for your story, your true cause needs to be told.
In all of you, that core of meaning must be exposed
so when the wind drops, and you sit by the Shee Water
doubting yourself, waiting for a fresh delivery of breath

for a moment, linger by its bustling mystery, reflecting
its intent with a gathering of words, and across it
a skim of the Cateran's history will dance quietly past
in and out of your brief yet growing respected presence

and the faces of your own warriors will appear about you.
The lines of their stories merging with the slow ripples
where your cupped hands break the surface but still clear:
their berets, their uniforms - their whole rig will become you.

Raise your sights!

For there it is. The answer to those mocking, muscle bound
mountains, whose only intention was to expose your fears,
and to echo the loose doubts escaping from your heads.
There it is, the only answer. You're here for your own warriors.

And then behind you, the bark of a puzzled old ewe
will break the respected hush with a call to arms.
All that you need think of is reduced to the lasting reflection
of faces strengthening you, urging you on to the finish.

The mountains will still mock, still posture but respectfully
and will seem less of a threat. Their stony arms unfolding,
lighter, almost welcoming. The scree path will tighten,
where the cold finger on your shoulder has let you go

and will guide you onwards with your back to the slopes
where Griz an Cateran fades irrelevant, surrendered where
this ancient noble landscape widens into a smile knowing
the tales of the brave in your heart will bring you safely home.

Viral

The birdsong seems unbalanced
in amongst the digger rumble, or
is it my understanding of tone?

At once urgent then flat, perhaps
our common bond, to ignore the churn
of scrub and diversion of waters

which we've taken for granted
forever, for nothing – nothing left
but naked history, the layers

bleaching in weak winter sun
grateful for the mizzle kiss the clouds
offer up in sympathy, in a fold

downwards of tears, unable to control
ravages of progress – our unquestioned
need for constructed space gone viral.

Hooks

February is the child of a wayward Summer
raised with attitude
that taunts Winter's frosted discipline
and stifles rebellious colours
when it's uncertain of their precise intentions.

It shuffles about the beginning of the year
holding up the other months, fidgeting,
without a to-do list, never
has the correct change of weather to hand
but frankly doesn't give a solid fat ball what you think.

Its breath is damp, bruised, slumped
and puddles into the same mucous spun web
with no regard for the frail hours
dutifully attending its scribbled whims.

Even the crows
are wary of it. For weeks, they've scolded
and mocked Winter's efforts
from their skeletal buttress, with
their high altered snobbery
but are now hunkered down, resigned
exhausted, content to surrender yet
willing the light opening its shoulders
above them to thicken the air.

An air bringing the scent of hope,
of hyacinth barely visible but
it's there, casting soft hooks
from its neat blue, chaliced rows
daring to risk birth on a mouldy bed
of birch bone and feathered stain.

You can smell it. It's there in smears,
of snow in the salt wind coiling,
looping around the hooks, tempting
and gently scratching at the soft,
exposed underbelly of your thoughts
where the tease of a resurrection
will unfold from under the blanket
when February has bored itself of you
- moved on.

Unscripted

I can even hear the river
its way of passing unnoticed
slowly down through days
purging the stale winter choke
opening up the spring light
and underneath, in the turn
where the tide takes a stand
bracing a shoulder to the weight
the fish cry out
but the silt muffles their plea.

I listen for the willows, leaning
into the shifting vein-like skim
on days when I'm alone
and their words become clear
and their sadness overwhelms
the urgency of my breathless hours.

I hear the clouds unclip, let loose
and it all becomes life
where the buds blink
where the grass inhales
where the merle sings
it becomes a choir
a season ticket
it becomes
a new mystery, unscripted
tempting us to love again.

If only we could resist
but we won't
a little love, unplanned
is not so bad.

What matters is
climbing out of the sadness.
I was born for this.

I was born to find heaven's gems
before they're lost to the sea.

Twa Chiels
For Aileen

We shared the shift of fresh water ash
where the Ericht's down-tumble slows
catching the brace of the crumbling kerb
where the bairns of my days took a dook
or ran summer rapids in inflated tyre tubes
with innocent daftness splashing the sun.

We shared the space, pencil & word weaving
soft stitches through river skim, birch bone,
nebbin stone checked by the dipper's urgency
& we were content, common-art bonded
to let our endeavours drift in the mizzle
tak a dook in the shallow bustle to the Brig

maybe to nudge up against the old lad wedged
on the weir, gnarled, weary & bleached praying
for a heft of snow melt to help him on his way, or
maybe to wait for us to return another bonded day
to polish our words, fill in sketchbook outlines
or perhaps add more colour to the old kirk window.

Spirit

Yer like a wee spuggy noo.
Still bonny but mair rickle than ah mind.
A flichtless angel fidgetin aboot in this hoose
ower dark, set in the wids, ower mossy
in the birk scrub. Aince ah thocht
it was a palace fou o mountains,
wi endless roads unner corniced skies,
whaur stars clustered intae chandelier cakes.

Stars which noo seem ower mauchless,
no able tae ignite yer sperkle.
The ane which wid erupt at ony meenit,
spiral intae a clatterin flame
an tak me oan a dance o joy
aboot the room, bumpin aa daft
intae the sofa, turnin the scowl
oan yon scary green wumman
ower the mantelpiece intae a reluctant smile.

But noo, in yer best frock,
they've pasted oot yer sperkle, yer een
closed tae them, but no tae me.
Ah ken yer in there. Ah ken yer in me, wi yer wings
unfolded, chucklin at aa the fuss.
Will ye wave back, or tap oot the rhythm
if ah hae anither wee go at makin
the green wummin laugh? Ah pray so,
fir aa eh ever wanted wis fir ye tae flee

A Freshwater Kiss

Footsteps of freshwater
paced out across the polished scrape
where the rumble of stones
underscores the journey.

I pick out my steps
slipping on the edge of the froth.
The urgency of the river
spills in and out of the bend.

A buzzard checks my progress
with the countenance of a shepherd
and folds into the pine canopy.
The famine of winter, distant.

The edge of the river, moss-stoned
forgives my intrusion, settling
under the canopy of birch bone.
Glenshee exhales the kiss of sun.

Hard

hard, very hard
word to word combat
with no faces to judge defeat
too long in trenches
we dissolve into ponds

she should have kept speaking
she should have kept breathing
she should have found words

why did they take away her words?

they could've fed her letters, syllables even

but they filled her mouth with pebbles
polished smooth, no fate prescribed
not that it mattered, in death

she didn't weigh much
when she fell silent, rolled
into a white sheet

the bed empty for a moment
until the queue shuffles up one

and the mortuary has a radio
Play for Today, words at peace
with the settle of strangers
easy, so very easy

Floral Printed Axe
After Selma

I am not of the machine. I
am not anonymous. I
am a woman. I survive.
I live my day in the hours
one by one, to make a life
bearable so I can be tomorrow.
I wear a pretty dress to be comfortable
to make a living, not
to be of the machine, not
to be anonymous. I can wield an axe
to the machine, to the discarded
here in the space we share
where the veins of humanity
in cadavers of steel and plastic
become knotted, in clusters
and strands which pull us together
between the hypnotic call,
of the golden neon M, stripping, sanitising
and the polished, sharp purpose
of my axe, dismantling, cleaving
separating the worthless from
the worth. I stand, in between metaphors
my aesthetic muscles exploding
through floral printed limbs and power through
teasing gently freedom from oppression
from your boundaries, from my terra nullius
where skin is trashed and I aim for the core

for its drumbeat heart. I am all yours
on the square, vulnerable, yet not tortured,
not chained, not for your entertainment.
I am all mine in the sweep of air, down
with the axe, with my ancestors willing me
into the ache of the machine. Its entrails
splayed for all to feed from yet
I am not of you. I never can be.
I am not of the machine.
I never will be.

The Knock

The cold slip of bogged down sand finds my feet again.
I remember all of the falsehoods laid neatly in open disguise
on the dashboard, with unrehearsed guilt
the unravelling of loves, the confessions
of his misadventures offered in the note
on the passenger seat.

I was alone
where it is neither ground or sea, standing
by his marinated death, a crumpled splay
of denim, tweed
and a crown of wrack:
seagulls looping slow-winged mournful coils,
the tide unfolding its black lace in questionable respect.

He had sat in the car
alone, the whisky exhaling in the cheap glass
the doctor's words blocking, but the pen steady
on an uncertain tide waiting for one more sentence
for it all to make sense, rehearsing its drama for when

the moment is now, a treacled confusion
pointless emotion wading past the detritus
of getting by, bundled memories left out
for recycling, the pram from lost walks abandoned,
the smell of chips cooking, welcoming you, hating you
through the blistered door where a child cries
at the knocks, a triple knock

but a single blow
to disparate lives spiralling down
into a numbing void of his consequence, his words
only words but be prepared for each one.
A hot coal will liquify the membranes of innocent lives
In the spew of cobbled together emotions
thinly disguised as sympathy –

you're husband's dead

And here now
the tide has found its recoil
free from the unrehearsed guilt
at peace with its part in the intrusion

and I watch the gulls gather
and I drink from the empty glass
and the sea recedes from me into the night.
The cold slip of bogged down sand finds my feet again.

James
A King in Waiting

What's that you say?
You've decided to find me?
I straighten up as best I can and listen to your plan
to bring me into your new found burst of energy,
into your digital environment with all its trimmings
of likes, and follows, of lottery hope
and bonus ball polemics. Not that I'm lost, but
simply forgotten to you and your business of getting by
whilst under generations of damp history, layered in soil
broken crockery, broken lives I suffocate this seal of concrete.
I open an eye occasionally when I hear my name
being mentioned and it worms its way in to me,
to tease my spirit but I have become used to false dawns
to the glimpses of justice promised then discarded
in school jotters, and the odd exam paper then I
panic, another threat to my puggled bones, scattered
enough by the heft of industry above me in the dark
rumble of time passing which I know nothing about
other than the strain it has put in the space between
my skull and the spread of ribs where my heart
still beats in its case of earth – a pillow of damp expectation.

Dear reader, I beg of you. Let not history nor circumstance
break your resolve. Let the last words of your determination
be mine and I will give up my unanointed hollow
if you will find me a place to rest where I can shake off
the mould of time and the stench of their murderous act
which clings to my soul.

I ask only this of you.

I am a spirit with many pasts but with no future.

I am a King in waiting.

Finish Your Brew

Let's go up the quarry path, but not yet -
finish your brew first - hot tea comfort
in a mug - happy to please your cold hands.

It'll not matter the sun has slipped
and the snell turn of the wind
has sneaked under the back door.

It'll not matter the clouds have slumped
and the day has accepted its purpose –
stitching yesterday to tomorrow.

We'll walk the path together, counting
geese with our good fortune tucked
safely in cosy pockets of hot tea blessings.

The Landing

This was the landing.
This was the whole space
but you will ask where are the drowned voices,
the bleached shells filled with ocean song
and the rain that tapped out the long hours
for our words to curve the dunes
with misadventure and the folly of open hearts.

Here the opening buds catch the first spray,
rise up and unburden in stifled air
like frosted glass crumbling, forgotten
in the loosened fuss of the first tide.

Here the machair fidgets endlessly, holding
grains that shift and shift then drum-beat
tone-soft to whisper tough truths into the sun's
withering scrutiny conjured out of nothing.

So remember it all, the landing,
the call of choirs assembling
under feather weave and hawk-bit cushion
and listen for the incoming fold
accept the consequence
and we will find all we need
to try again tomorrow.

Take the Skite

the bother wi scrievin's muckle hard
maist fowk strive ower much fer glories
reachin yon stratosphere withoot regard
breathin life in tae their nurtured stories
an takin puir sustenance fae the icy glare
o proonach publicity o social media might
but wha can sustain sic a fragile hope
fir scarfin fear at least o a genteel skite
or worse, danglin fae the rejection rope?

yet the risks drive us blindly oan
despite alarm bells ringin wi sense
but muffled by oor gallus thrawn
tae fester, an vanish in the dense
body o ithers opinions, wha's
beeks an shairpened claws
gather oan the neebourin wa's
tae scavenge gleeful oan rank deflation
aince yer spurned by a fickle Nation

Blame

My call slips in silence
over the mountains.

Despite the full moon
on the crackle glaze, why
am I to blame for the shadows?

A tone in voice and gesture
is all I have left
for tomorrow's rain. Why

won't you embrace it? Must
you always arrive too late
to embrace my light.

Bind

Time scuds forrit, bruising thin days.
Not stopping for the chiel struggling
to keep up, to make sense of it all.

Loneliness. Such a hollowed out cave
Shaped by the chaos of life, pebbles
of self-loathing working into soft walls.

Like poisoned ivy, it binds itself to the solid,
Makes ghosts of futures, mutes the words
of lovers & pulls at the out-stretched hand.

What a burden to overcome! Beyond imagining.
Time will hurry on but for a moment step off
to one side, let it pass. Look for the alone.

ABOUT THE AUTHOR

Jim Mackintosh was born and lives in Perthshire, Scotland. He has had five collections of poetry published, the last being **The Rubicon of Ash** in 2016. That same year, Jim became the 'Poet in Residence' for St Johnstone F.C., the first professional football club in Scotland to make such an appointment. Through the residency Jim became involved in various community projects one of which culminated in him editing the highly acclaimed anthology **Mind the Time** published in aid of the dementia support charity Football Memories Scotland.

In 2018, Jim was the 'Poet in Residence' for the Perthshire-based arts festival **Platform**.

Jim is also an active member of the committees of The Friends of Hugh Miller, The Friends of William Soutar, and the Blairgowrie-based festival, Hamish Matters, which aims to keep Hamish Henderson's legacy alive in the place of his birth.

ABOUT THE TYPEFACE

The history of the realist sans-serif known today as DIN goes back to 1905. At the time, the Prussian railway created a set of lettering with the purpose of unifying the descriptions on their freight cars. Following a merger of all German state railways in 1920, the master drawings of the Prussian railway became the reference for most railway lettering. Based on the master drawings, the D. Stempel AG foundry released the earliest version of a DIN face in 1923.

The typeface was adopted by Germany in 1936 as a standard known as DIN 1451 (DIN is an acronym for Deutsches Institut für Normung—in English, the German Institute for Standardisation). The typeface became a standard for traffic signs, street signs, house numbers, and licence plates. Over the next decades the typeface also found use on various household goods and products, making it synonymous with German design.

In 1995, type designer Albert-Jan Pool expanded DIN 1451 into a more polished form acceptable for graphic design and publishing, known as FF DIN. It is this version which has been used in this book.

[*Extracted from "Know Your Type" blog on idsgn.org*]

THE PUBLISHER

Tippermuir Books Ltd (*est.* 2009) is an independent publishing company based in Perth, Scotland.

OTHER TITLES FROM TIPPERMUIR BOOKS

Spanish Thermopylae (Paul S. Philippou, 2009)

Battleground Perthshire
(Paul S. Philippou & Robert A. Hands, 2009)

Perth: Street by Street
(Paul S. Philippou & Roben Antoniewicz, 2012)

Born in Perthshire
(Paul S. Philippou & Robert A. Hands, 2012)

In Spain with Orwell (Christopher Hall, 2013)

Trust (Ajay Close, 2014)

Perth: As Others Saw Us (Donald Paton, 2014)

Love All (Dorothy L. Sayers, 2015)

A Chocolate Soldier (David W. Millar, 2016)

The Early Photographers of Perthshire
(Roben Antoniewicz & Paul S. Philippou, 2016)

Taking Detective Novels Seriously:
The Collected Crime Reviews of Dorothy L. Sayers
(Dorothy L. Sayers and Martin Edwards, 2017)

Walking with Ghosts (Alan J. Laing, 2017)

No Fair City: Dark Tales From Perth's Past
(Gary Knight, 2017)

The Tale o the Wee Mowdie that
wantit tae ken wha keeched on his heid
(Werner Holzwarth and Wolf Erlbruch,
translated by Matthew Mackie, 2017)

Hunters: Wee Stories from the Crescent:
A Reminiscence of Perth's Hunter Crescent
(Anthony Camilleri, 2017)

Perth: Scott's Fair City –
The Fair Maid of Perth & Sir Walter Scott –
A Celebration & Guided Tour
(Paul S. Philippou, with
Roben Antoniewicz and Rob Hands, 2018)

FORTHCOMING

The Scots Emoji Dictionary (Michael Dempster, 2018)

A Perth & Kinross Miscellany (Trish Conlon, 2018)

All titles are available from
bookshops and online booksellers.

They can also be purchased directly at
www.tippermuirbooks.co.uk

Tippermuir Books Ltd can be contacted at
mail@tippermuirbooks.co.uk